# Praying for Purpose
## for women

# Praying for Purpose

## for women

a prayer
experience that
will change your
life forever

# Katie Brazelton

**ZONDERVAN®**

**ZONDERVAN.com/**
**AUTHORTRACKER**
*follow your favorite authors*

 **ZONDERVAN®**

*Praying for Purpose for Women*
Copyright © 2005 by Katherine F. Brazelton

Requests for information should be addressed to:

Zondervan, *Grand Rapids, Michigan* 49530

Softcover edition: 978-0-310-29284-5

---

**Library of Congress Cataloging-in-Publication Data**

Brazelton, Katie, 1950–
    Praying for purpose for women : a prayer experience that will change your life forever /
Katie Brazelton.
        p. cm. – (The pathway to purpose series)
    Includes bibliographical references.
    ISBN   978-0-310-25652-6 (hardcover)
        1. Christian women—Prayer-books and devotions—English.  2. Christian women—Religious
life.  3. Prayer—Christianity.  4. Vocation—Christianity.  I. Title. II. Series.
    BV4844.B735 2005
    248.8'43—dc22                                                                        2004024103

08  09  10  11  12  13  ·  20  19  18  17  16  15  14  13  12  11  10  9  8  7  6  5  4  3  2  1

*In loving memory of my mom,*
*Rosalie Marie Murphy,*
*who was my dear friend and*
*a godly prayer warrior.*

*To my sweet dad and family members.*
*You pray with passion, purpose,*
*and expectancy.*

*Thank you for what you have taught me*
*about prayer, love, and ministry.*

# CONTENTS

Part Two
## INVITING THE HOLY SPIRIT TO REVEAL
## YOUR LIFE PURPOSES

# How to Use the Pathway to Purpose Series

All three Pathway to Purpose books work together to enhance your journey as you discover your unique God-given calling.

*Pathway to Purpose for Women*, the main book in the series, shows you how to connect your to-do list, your passions, and God's purposes for your life. How do you live through—see through—the *ordinary* when you yearn for your own *significant* purpose? Discover how God has uniquely designed you and used your life experiences to prepare you for your specific calling. If you can read only one of the three books, this is the one to read. (This book also is available as an Abridged Audio CD.)

- *Personal use*—Each chapter ends with a Bible exploration and personal questions.
- *Small Group and Retreat use*—See the Group Discussion Guide in the back of the book.

*Conversations on Purpose for Women* is designed for the reader of *Pathway to Purpose for Women* who wants to go deeper. This workbook encourages you to choose a Purpose

Partner and make ten appointments with each other. Enjoy conversation starters, Scripture verses, questions, and specific self-assessment exercises that help you unpack God's unique purpose for your life, from an initial sneak preview to the most challenging steps of your journey.

- *Personal use with your Purpose Partner*—Find a partner and enjoy fellowship and growth while exploring God's specific life purposes together.
- *Small Group and Retreat use*—Work through the book as a small group, women's Sunday school class, or in a retreat setting by dividing into groups of three to four maximum and completing and discussing the exercises at paced intervals.

*Praying for Purpose for Women* is a sixty-day prayer experience that guides you as you ask God to reveal your life's purposes. You will discover insights from modern-day role models and biblical characters, specific questions to ask yourself as you seek God's answers, and an eye-opening analysis of your life patterns and purposes.

- *Personal use*—This book can be used by itself as a daily devotional. However, if you use it as a devotional while reading *Pathway to Purpose for Women*, your whole experience will be deepened and solidified.
- *Retreat use*—Ideal for a solitude retreat. Women can work through the book at their own pace during the weekend. On the last day together, they can pair up to discuss their findings, regardless of how far they got in the book.

Also available:

*Pathway to Purpose for Women Personal Journal*

As you search for and discover God's unique purpose for your life, it is important to record "what the Lord has done" in your family life, your personal life, and your ministry life. Each page in this companion book to *Pathway to Purpose for Women* will guide your journaling and allow you to reflect on how God is directing you on the pathway of your life.

And I urge you to consider this supplemental material:

*The Purpose Driven® Life*

My dear pastor, Rick Warren, wrote this phenomenal best-seller, which sends up a clarion call for people to live out God's five purposes for their lives. If you haven't read his book yet, I highly recommend it. I also recommend that your church go through the powerful 40 Days of Purpose campaign.

# Series Foreword

In 1997 Katie facilitated a two-day Life Plan for me and I found the experience highly significant—a turning point!

Up until then, I had been frustrated and confused about my spiritual gifts and goals, and unclear about the contribution my life would make for God's kingdom. Through Katie's firm-yet-gentle guidance, I viewed my life with new eyes and discovered a greater appreciation for God. Using large sheets of butcher paper hanging in her living room, we traced the path I had taken from childhood, and it became crystal-clear that God had been directing me at every point. I was humbled and convinced of his love for me. Things I knew intellectually moved from my head to my heart, and I was able to find joy and meaning in pain I had experienced.

The Holy Spirit used Katie to open my eyes to attitudes, sins, and wrong desires that I had been holding on to, and through a healing prayer time, I was able to release them. After reviewing the past and confirming the present, she drew from me the blue-sky dreams I had for my future . . . dreams I had been afraid to say out loud. In Katie's warm, gracious, encouraging presence, I invited God to use me in ways I never expected, never thought possible, and never even dared to hope. Our tears mingled as she affirmed God's call on my life, her belief that God had allowed the pain for his good purposes, and her faith in my ability to actually fulfill the God-inspired goals and dreams articulated in our time together.

Years later, many of those lessons still affect my daily life. God has taken me up on my offer to be used by him, and though the task often seems more than I can handle, I think back to those hours of breakthrough and am reassured that HE is directing my steps and HE will finish the work.

Katie brings this same warmth, gentle firmness, deep conviction, and passion for God to her books. You may never have the privilege of calling her "friend" as I do, but through her writings, you will find a dear companion for your spiritual journey.

Kay Warren
Saddleback Church
November 2004

Part One

# Praying God's Purposes for Your Life

For the next sixty days, absorb the wisdom of God's Word and the wisdom of a wide cross-section of Christian women who will share with you their journey on the pathway to purpose. As you do, pray intentionally for the Lord to direct you on your own specific journey.

# Your Divine Appointments with God

Welcome to *Praying for Purpose for Women*. This sixty-day prayer experience is designed to help you answer the question: *What hopes, longings, passions, strengths, character, faith, and values did God instill in me for his use, his glory, and his purposes?* Yes, you do have a purpose beyond all the really hard years of going to school, accomplishing your to-do lists, and building a retirement fund! If you truly desire God's greatest plans for your present and future, the most powerful things you can do are to pray, reflect on Scripture, read about biblical and modern-day role models, take time to listen to God as he mentors you about his wishes, and record your insights. This book will coach you daily to do that.

## An Overview: Where You're Headed

In this prayer experience you will accomplish five important things:

1. *Become an eyewitness to purpose in the lives of others* by reading sixty surprising interviews of Christian women role models and sixty stories about Bible characters.

2. *Uncover purpose in your life* by answering sixty tough and insightful questions that will lead you to a clearer understanding of who God formed you to be.

3. *Pray for purpose* by praying sixty specific Scripture prayers for life direction and by taking the time to listen for God's answers.

4. *Summarize purpose* by evaluating your life themes, patterns, and action steps, and by having your written comments reviewed by a dear friend or spouse, who will tell you the truth about what she/he notices.

5. *Live out purpose in your life* by consistently completing your own prayerfully recommended action steps.

Part 1 will focus on who God is, how much he loves you, and how uniquely he created you. You will see that you are only a steward of the personality, roles, and talents he has entrusted to you. You will explore topics related to your time, money, resources, energy, character, ministry, brokenness, successes, network, and platform, among others, as each affects the kingdom-building mission for which you were born.

Each day features the response of an influential woman to one of sixty critical questions about life purpose. When you read these behind-the-scenes and, sometimes, never-before-heard stories—explaining how these women slowly and often painstakingly grew into God's plan for their lives—you will see that they are just like you, facing issues similar to your own. Not one of them has been exempt from life's struggles and not one of them has all the answers. In other words, the barrier between the women who appear to have it all together and the rest of us who often feel like we are floundering *does not exist.*

In Part 2, you will record your life themes and patterns, "connecting the dots" about things you may not have understood before. And, most importantly, you will answer two key questions:

1. From what you notice—even if they don't seem logical to you right now—what appear to be your current life purposes?
2. From what you notice—even if it doesn't seem logical to you right now—what appears to be your unique, passionate ache that God instilled in your heart before you were born?

Answers to these questions will free you up to enjoy doing "today things" today and prayerfully preparing for your tomorrows!

## How to Get the Most Out of This Prayer Book

- *Take your time.* I suggest that you read through only one lesson per day for sixty days, so that you won't attempt to rush through your prayers and reflections for the sake of getting answers sooner. This process takes time.
- *Pray personally.* When you see a blank line in the Suggested Prayer, fill in your first name on the line to personalize your prayer. In that way, you will actually be praying Scripture back to God. Remember to keep your Bible handy to read about each day's Bible character.

- *Trust the process.* I can't promise you that you will like (or understand) the progression of the questions as you move through the book. The seemingly random order of the questions (and some redundancy) clears itself up during Part 2, when you slot your answers into categories. To dwell on this ahead of time could skew your response or dwarf your insights. Just enjoy the process, trust the Holy Spirit, and don't try to figure everything out.
- *Dig deep.* I suggest that you *not use the same words* to answer more than two questions. This will cause you to dig deeper for truths or to, at least, phrase your answer from a different perspective.
- *Welcome the struggle.* If you find yourself asking, *Why is this question challenging me?* allow yourself the freedom to be uncomfortable as God confronts you with any truth he would like you to hear. You may even need to deeply ponder your answer throughout the day as you talk to him about your feelings (anger, sadness, fear, elation, surprise, curiosity, or other). Figuratively speaking, ask him to open your eyes, just like he did literally for the blind man, Bartimaeus (see Mark 10:46–52).
- *Desire a change in your life.* Let the process stir up a persistent desire for a changed life that God will use. Anticipate that he will mobilize you now and in the future in a powerful way.
- *Let God mentor you.* Sit still and listen to him, so he can speak to you.

My intense longing for purpose in my own life—and my drive to learn of other women's struggles along this same path—sent me searching for answers around the world, when all along, my purpose was right before my eyes. May your decision to pray daily for purpose—for sixty days—help you be still, listen for God to speak, and see the magnificent purposes he has planned for you—that are right before your eyes. Enjoy these sixty divine appointments with God.

# WHAT ARE YOU AFRAID OF?

What is the first fear that jumps into your mind? We all struggle with fears, some paralyzing, others mildly nagging. What about you? What is your greatest fear? Fear can motivate you to seek God's strength and power, or it can keep you from embracing new opportunities, including those that would help you fulfill his plan for your life.

## YOU ARE NOT ALONE

I cross paths with women every day who have fears like these: heights, snakes, public speaking, cancer, terrorism, financial ruin, spiders, bridges, or dogs. Some have a fear of flying, falling, enclosed spaces, job loss, husband's death, being alone, fish, or chemical warfare. You may know someone who has a fear of abandonment, rejection, being attacked, failure, success, ridicule, or being found out that she's not smart. What about an extreme fear of dying, which causes you to avoid your annual checkup? Let's peek into the life of Michelle Akers, an Olympic soccer gold medalist, to see how she has wrestled with fear.

## MICHELLE AKERS WAS AFRAID

Michelle pursued and realized a successful career as an Olympian and world champion soccer player with the US women's national team. She spent fifteen years traveling around the world, living out of a suitcase, battling a serious illness (Chronic Fatigue and Immune Dysfunction Syndrome), and undergoing twenty-five surgeries on her knees, shoulder, and face. She is now retired and spends quality time with her husband, family and friends, horses, and Australian shepherd dogs. Michelle has a soft heart for kids going through difficult circumstances, and so she participates in several summer soccer camps.

Michelle recalls that her initial impression of Christians was that they were extremely judgmental, rigid in their behavior, and generally unimpressive in how they lived out their faith. But after a series of tragedies and tough circumstances, Michelle came to understand God's abundant love, grace, and goodness—and she chose to trust him with her life and heart. Michelle admits that she continues to struggle with a stubborn, independent streak, but for the most part, she is holding steady to the road that God has chosen for her and relies daily on the strength and courage he provides her.

As Michelle stood on the gold medal platform after the 1996 Atlanta games and acknowledged the stadium full of cheering crowds and media, she felt that God was saying, "To whom much is given, much is required." He impressed upon her the vastness of his chosen sphere of influence for her. She understood that her assignment was to inspire and encourage people who were struggling through difficult life circumstances, especially those who wondered what their purpose was and how they were going to make it through another day. Since then, she has been determined to implant the Joshua 1:9 promise ("God will be with you") in as many hearts as possible.

Michelle's greatest, unrelenting fear has been that she will get her heart broken. Some rough family relationships set the stage for disappointment and broken trust. After much counseling, she is learning to put this fear behind her. Now, she has a deeper understanding of her relationship with God and with her husband, who "would outrun a herd of wild horses and wrestle six lions to be sure she was loved and safe."

Michelle sums up her feelings by saying: "With God's promise to be with me echoing loud and clear every day of my life, there is nothing too big, too terrible, too strong, or too disappointing for me to overcome."

**What Are You Afraid Of?**

**The Israelite Spies Were Afraid**

Twelve spies were sent to explore the land of Canaan. Ten of them came back and instilled fear into the hearts of the Israelites with their reports of giants in the land. Only Caleb and Joshua were courageous. Read Numbers 13–14. If you had been one of the spies, would you have been described as courageous or fearful?

## SCRIPTURE TO PONDER

*The LORD said . . . "Have I not commanded you? Be strong and courageous. Do not be terrified; do not be discouraged, for the LORD your God will be with you wherever you go." (Joshua 1:1, 9)*

## SUGGESTED PRAYER

*Dear Lord, you want me, _____ [your first name], to be strong and courageous. You said, "Do not be terrified; do not be discouraged, for the LORD your God will be with you wherever you go." Today I pray that I will learn to trust you more and more. Help me track my progress toward freedom from fear, so that I can always remember how far you've brought me. I thank you in advance for delivering me from my fears.*

### So . . . What Insight, Prayer, or Action Step Has God Laid on Your Heart Today?

_____

_____

_____

_____

_____

_____

_____

# WHAT CONSEQUENCES HAVE YOU FACED FROM A LIFE MISTAKE?

Have you paid a costly price for one of your mistakes? Did you learn your lesson fairly quickly, or were you one of God's more stubborn students? Today is as good a day as any to press the pause button on your life and take stock of your past consequences. Doing so can prevent similar, future consequences that could delay God's plan for your life.

## ONCE YOU'VE BEEN THERE, YOU NEVER WANT TO GO BACK

Have you faced consequences like debt, broken trust, or a ruined reputation? Have you dealt with consequences such as bitterness, illness, someone's death, addiction, lost wages, or rumors? Have you faced hatred, guilt, shame, regrets, missed opportunities, or the need for forgiveness? Have you lost your joy, needed to repent and to pay retribution, had your freedom taken away, or faced delays? Jill Savage, author of *Professionalizing Motherhood*, tells how consequences for her actions taught her about truth.

## JILL SAVAGE'S CONSEQUENCES
## WERE NOT SO INCONSEQUENTIAL

Jill founded Hearts at Home, an organization that encourages women in the profession of motherhood. She is a passionate speaker and the author of three books on motherhood, marriage, and mom's groups. Married twenty years, she and her husband Mark have five children and are helping to start a church in central Illinois.

When Jill was nineteen, she clearly remembers the movement she made away from religion toward a personal relationship with Jesus Christ. She is deeply grateful for the truth God shared with her at that time and for its relevance and impact on her life.

After having two children, she felt led by God to give up her beloved career as a music teacher and to stay home with a joy-filled spirit to raise her family. She came to understand that life purposes don't always show up in big ways announced by fanfare, but are often right in front of us in the daily arenas of life. She discovered, for example, that ministering to her husband and children is among the most important and precious life purposes she has. After some transitional time in her new season of life, God asked Jill to encourage other wives and mothers to more thoroughly enjoy their roles.

Jill knows that she wasn't always a likely candidate for such a huge assignment from God. When she began her role as a wife, she had a critical, judgmental spirit. Her husband's emotionally unhealthy childhood made it very easy for her to blame him for their problems, despite his protests. This robbed their early marriage of its life and love. Then she learned to apply Matthew 7:5 to her life: "You hypocrite, first take the log out of your own eye, and then you will see clearly to take the speck out of your brother's eye" (NASB). Over time, her marriage turned around. She believes that God allowed her another chance because he wanted her to tell others about his incredible mercy.

She warns: "You will experience painful consequences as long as you live outside of God's truth. My marriage, for example, was damaged by my sin, until the unbearable consequences drove me to truth."

**What Consequences Have You Faced from a Life Mistake?**

**Zechariah Faced Consequences**

Zechariah was not able to speak until the eighth day after his son was born, because he had not believed the words of the angel Gabriel. Zechariah's consequences were severe, but he definitely learned his lesson. Read Luke 1:5–68. How do you feel about severe consequences?

## Scripture to Ponder

*But your iniquities have separated you from your God;*
*your sins have hidden his face from you, so that he will not hear.*
*(Isaiah 59:2)*

## Suggested Prayer

*Dear Lord my God, so that my iniquities do not separate me from you; so that my sins will not cause you to hide your face from me and not hear me, I, _____, want to tell you how sorry I am for my sins. Please forgive me today and shower me with unmerited grace. Thank you that you, as my good and loving Father, discipline me. Help me grow more than I could ever imagine through consequences that are sent by or allowed by you. Only you offer freedom, healing, hope, and a secure future—before, during, and after the necessary consequences. And, for those consequences I have faced that were not caused by sin in my life, thank you for seeing me through.*

**So . . . What Insight, Prayer, or Action Step Has God Laid on Your Heart Today?**

_____

_____

_____

_____

_____

_____

_____

_____

# WHEN HAVE
# YOU PERSEVERED?

What took long-term stamina for you to accomplish? Are you glad you did not give up? How often did your mind wage war against your emotions, saying, *I can't do this anymore; yes I can; no I can't; I'm not quitting*? But you kept at it. You persevered to the end! You were rewarded with what you set out to accomplish. Did you notice that your character improved along the way? God has assigned to you certain purposes in life for which he expects loyalty and commitment. The attitude that grows through perseverance is, *There's no turning back from what God asks!*

## PERSEVERANCE IS NOT OPTIONAL

Was there a time in your life when giving up was not an option? Perhaps God asked you to restore a relationship, build a ministry, heal from abuse, forgive an offender, or find a job. Maybe he entrusted you to raise a terrible-twos toddler, pray for an unsaved spouse, be a good witness during a serious illness, or wait patiently for a book contract. Did you persevere while completing your undergraduate degree, learning to play racquetball, finalizing an adoption, or building a cabin? Florence Littauer, founder of CLASS (Christian Leaders, Authors, and Speakers Services), continues to persevere for God.

## Florence Littauer Doesn't Give Up

Florence is the author of thirty books on topics such as encouragement, relationships, and communication. Many of her titles have sold more than a hundred thousand copies each; *Personality Plus* has sold more than a million. She has received an Honorary Doctorate of Humanities, has been a member of the National Speakers' Association for twenty years, and has been chosen for the Award for Excellence from her peers.

Florence dearly loves to study God's Word, live it, and teach others to live it. She taught her daughter, Marita, that leaders are servants of God and that they do whatever it takes to help out, including sweeping floors in an auditorium before a keynote speech. Florence has changed the world of Christian speaking. Through her commitment of twenty-three years of leadership, she has trained more than ten thousand men and women by giving them the tools and techniques of effective communication.

Florence describes how difficult persevering can be: "Writing one book per year, sometimes two, for the past twenty-five years has not been an easy task. At one point, I had fast-approaching deadlines for a book, a Bible study, and a line of greeting cards, but each day there was something that distracted me from writing. It is only through the grace of God and his gift to me of disciplined perseverance, despite delays, that I met those deadlines and will meet others in the future. Praise God for his grace and his gift."

Her secret strategy: "Pray and decide where you believe God wants you to be ten years from now, and then ... get on with it! Say, 'Yes, I can. Yes, I will. Yes, I am starting right now.' And, remember, the first step is always the hardest one of all."

**When Have You Persevered?**

**A Widow Understood the Virtue of Perseverance**

Jesus told a parable about a widow who, because of her persistence, was finally granted justice by an evil judge. This story about persistence will remind you to pray continually with expectant faith. Read the parable in Luke 18:1–8. Who do you know who has been worn out or beaten down, but didn't give up?

## SCRIPTURE TO PONDER

*Not only so, but we also rejoice in our sufferings, because we know that suffering produces perseverance; perseverance, character; and character, hope.*
*(Romans 5:3–4)*

## SUGGESTED PRAYER

*Dear Lord, help me, _____, learn to rejoice in my*
*sufferings, because I know that suffering produces perseverance;*
*perseverance, character; and character, hope. Today I pray that*
*I will become a woman of extreme perseverance, not letting*
*difficulties and delays discourage me. I ask especially for*
*persistence that will build my character and give me hope when*
*I am in a "holding pattern" of waiting for things to happen or*
*improve. Help me see that it is actually easier for me to persevere*
*than to live with the regret of having given up hope. Thank you*
*for your gift of perseverance.*

### So . . . What Insight, Prayer, or Action Step Has God Laid on Your Heart Today?

# What's Confused in Your Life?

Have you ever been so confused about something that it literally made you sick? Has confusion clouded your judgment? Many women mask their pain of confusion to the world. They put on makeup and a stoic face. They don a smart-looking outfit and a matching demeanor. They sip their coffee and zip their lips, never daring to let on that they are creatures of confusion. Go ahead and admit today that there is something in your life that confuses you. It will set you free from that world of secrets and invite God's clarity and purpose. One bit of advice: Until God speaks, wait to take action.

## Confusion Reigns Supreme!

What's your greatest area of confusion? Is it whether to be an entrepreneur, how to deal with coworker cliques, when to downsize for retirement, or how to stop the grumbling in your ministry? Does your confusion have to do with your medical debt, waning spirituality, management style, life balance, or time-consuming hobby? Do you wonder where you are supposed to plant seeds of faith, how to de-clutter your home and garage, or what to do about someone who is slandering you? Are you confused about a love relationship; a child's mysterious, lingering illness; or a career move? Are you confused about who to trust, what to do next, or why you were blamed for something? Anita Renfroe, a retreat worship leader and humorist, is a self-proclaimed confused woman!

## ANITA RENFROE DOES THE DAILY-NESS DANCE WITH CONFUSION

Anita is a comedian, songwriter, and artist who uses comedy to spread the joy of Jesus, touching the funny bone on her way to the heart. She calls herself a party waiting for a place to happen. She takes God very seriously, although she sees his humor everywhere! (She says, "Just focus on noses for a while—you'll see it too.") She rarely takes herself seriously.

Her calling is to get people to uncross their twisted-pretzel arms, unlock their tightly guarded emotions, and laugh at themselves. Anita says, "It's then that the Holy Spirit can break down the walls that divide us from each other and from God."

What's confused in Anita's life? She laughs, "What's *not* confused? Life, love, balance—I can't see my way clear on any of those issues! They seem to be in a tangle." Yet for Anita, this is a career plus, because all the things she feels confused about are fodder for her comedy. She understands how other people who don't have such a strange slant on life might find the confusion all too overwhelming, but she just grabs a microphone and talks about it.

She says, "Confusion is a direct result of the Fall. Up until then, life was, oh, so simple—so sparkling clear. Now we're all just trying to machete our way through the thicket that is this post-Eden, pre-Heaven, Earth-life. I am learning that, although God is not the author of confusion, he often uses the confusion in my life, so that I will listen more closely for his voice, examine more intently my past missteps, and appreciate more completely his peace that is only truly apparent in the middle of my muddle. I do strive, believe it or not, to stay in his presence, the only place where confusion is not a given on this confusing planet. Of course, since Earth is not our real home, the confusion makes us aliens and foreigners, who look all the more forward to arriving Home."

### What's Confused in Your Life?

### Simon of Cyrene Was Confused

Can you imagine the confusion of Simon of Cyrene, a man from North Africa who was conscripted at random by Roman guards to help Jesus carry his cross to Golgotha? Simon may still be saying, "And just how did that happen?" Read Mark 15:21. When have you found yourself saying, "And just how did that happen?" or "What am I supposed to do about that?"

44

## Scripture to Ponder

*If any of you lacks wisdom, he should ask God, who gives
generously to all without finding fault, and it will be given to him.*
(James 1:5)

## Suggested Prayer

*Dear Lord God, I, _____, lack wisdom and I ask you,
who gives generously to all without finding fault, to fill me
with wisdom. Your Word promises that you will do that for me.
I thank you for reminding me that I'm not alone in this life
quandary and that your light will clear up my confusion.
Help me hear your voice, your wisdom, your truth.*

**So . . . What Insight, Prayer, or Action Step
Has God Laid on Your Heart Today?**

_____

_____

_____

_____

_____

_____

_____

_____

_____

_____

# How Did God Use a Crisis or Problem to Bring Good into Your Life?

Recall one of the worst times of your life and the circumstances that surrounded it. Was it the death of a loved one, an unexpected divorce, or perhaps an eating disorder? Now go ahead and ask today's important question about the good that God was able to bring out of it. God will use all your troubles in his plan for your life—if you let him.

## No Shortage of Crises and Problems, No Shortage of God's Grace

What crisis or problem have you faced in your life: an addiction, infertility, a stock market crash, a kidnapping, an abortion, a job loss, an angry teen, or a hateful act of discrimination? How did God use your pain or sadness? Did he fill you with empathy for others, draw you closer to him, or teach you to obey him? Did it cause you to bond with someone more closely? Did you end up taking a risk you would not have taken? Did your grief or frustration turn you in a new direction, protect you from a greater harm, or give you wisdom you could share with others who were hurting? Did someone else ask you about your strong faith during your trials? Did you learn to trust God and let him help you? Janet Thompson, founder of Woman to Woman Mentoring, has seen God at work amidst her troubles.

## JANET THOMPSON WOULD NOT TRADE THE LESSONS SHE LEARNED

Janet is a well-known author and speaker on the topic of mentoring. Her *Woman to Woman Leader's Kit* for churches about how to start, grow, and maintain a mentoring ministry and her Bible study series *Mentoring God's Way* have enabled thousands of women around the world to experience the blessing of how two Christian women can walk side-by-side to help each other.

Janet says that she accepted Christ while attending a church camp at the age of ten. She eventually completed her Master's in Business Administration (MBA) that immersed her in the fast-paced corporate world, where she interacted primarily with men. In 1995, Janet heard God call her to "feed his sheep." He quickly revealed that *feeding* meant mentoring and that *his sheep*, in this case, were women, not men! To help prepare herself for this new work, she completed a Master's in Christian Leadership from Fuller Theological Seminary.

How did God use a crisis in Janet's life for good? Janet speaks and ministers to thousands of women every year and recalls that each time she was with a group of women, the thought would come to her, *Someone in this room will get breast cancer.* Then she would whisper, "Please, God, don't let it be me." But it *was* Janet in 2002, just as she was in the midst of a full speaking schedule; a demolished, unusable kitchen and living room being remodeled; the Christmas holidays; family coming to stay for three weeks; and her husband losing his job. Her experience with breast cancer in the middle of all that instability awakened in her a sense of deep compassion. She now understands the needs of someone in crisis and has learned all the things *not to say*. She was humbled by the focus on a private area of her body and by the mandatory requirement of accepting help. This, in turn, allows her to minister to others embarrassed by a delicate situation.

She says, "God will use our heartache, whatever its cause, to build our character, draw us closer to him, and make us pliable tools for his purposes. And, he will call on each of us from time to time to go through something, so we can better minister to others."

### How Did God Use a Crisis or Problem to Bring Good into Your Life?

### Joseph Had a Series of Crises that God Used for Good
Joseph, son of Jacob, was sold into slavery and later imprisoned, but that's not the whole story! Read Genesis 37:23–28; 39:1–19; 41:39; and 50:18–20. How do you think you would have fared if you were Joseph?

## SCRIPTURE TO PONDER

*And we know that in all things God works for the good of those who love him, who have been called according to his purpose. (Romans 8:28)*

## SUGGESTED PRAYER

*Dear Lord God, I, _____, know that in all things you work for the good of those who love you, those who have been called according to your purpose. Today I thank you for how you planned, in advance, to turn all my crises and problems into good—and that you have made that promise to all Christians. It gives me enormous hope. Help me always remember that you are my compassionate and caring Father. I give all my hurt and troubles to you to put to good use.*

### So . . . What Insight, Prayer, or Action Step Has God Laid on Your Heart Today?

# WHAT ARE A FEW
# OF YOUR TALENTS OR SKILLS?

God is aware of every single one of your talents and skills. In fact, he gave you all your godly ones at birth or helped you develop them along the way. It gives him great pleasure to see you use what you have been given. The first step in appreciating your talents and skills is recognizing them! Today is all about doing that, so you can dedicate them to the Lord for his service.

## TALENTS AND SKILLS? I DON'T HAVE ANY!

So, you are not a talented harpist, gifted communicator, or respected surgeon? But have people commented that you are a natural at cross-country skiing, landscape painting, or computer repairs? Do you even remember when you learned to be a stenographer, mechanic, or carpenter? Are you an incurable inventor, an avid researcher, or a party planner par excellence? Do you wonder why God gave you the gift of thinking clearly under pressure or of having a photographic memory? Have you mastered a foreign language or discovered that you have a special ability in an area like music, dance, graphics, problem solving, marketing, or supervising people? Sue Augustine, author of 5-*Minute Retreats for Women*, has a great perspective on using her best for God's glory.

## SUE AUGUSTINE APPRECIATES HER TALENTS AND SKILLS

After escaping eleven years of a physically abusive marriage and surviving a life-threatening illness, Sue began her incredible journey toward recovery. She now has an international speaking and writing career, through which she inspires others to make powerful, positive choices that will transform their lives.

Sue has been a Christian since giving her heart to the Lord nearly three decades ago. She reminisces about all the ministries she has served in over the years. She has been a Sunday-morning greeter, choir member, Sunday school and nursery school teacher, and church-camp counselor. She currently helps plan special outings, seasonal events, holiday dinners, game nights, and "pot-blessing" suppers for church members and their friends.

Sue encourages others through biblical insights and real-life examples. She shows people how to put life's trials into a heavenly perspective by facing each new challenge with grace and setting their sights on eternity. Sue shares her testimony with genuine empathy and compassion for others at retreats and conferences. She is clear about her life's current purpose: to bring new hope to those in seemingly hopeless situations and to encourage them to develop a closeness with God by trusting him fully.

Sue's talents include playing piano and watercolor painting, both of which help her to relax after a full travel schedule. Somewhere along the line, she realized that she loves to teach, to impart principles and techniques that motivate people to take action. And, her organizational skills led her to develop her best-selling seminar, *Organized & Clutter-Free At Last.*

She says, "Some of our abilities are God-given from birth and others are learned over many years of diligent practice. When we commit them all totally to the Lord, asking him daily to guide our every step in using them, we find true satisfaction."

**What Are a Few of Your Talents or Skills?**

_____

_____

_____

**A Man Was Given a Talent**
(In New Testament times, a talent was the largest unit of silver, with an approximate monetary value of one ox.) Jesus told a parable using a metaphor about a man who was rebuked by his master for burying his talent. Read Matthew 25:14–30. Today, let's extend the metaphor to include your natural talents and acquired skills. What would Jesus say to you? Are you using your talents and skills wisely or are you burying them?

_____

_____

_____

## SCRIPTURE TO PONDER

*Then the LORD said ... "And I have filled him with the Spirit of God, with skill, ability and knowledge in all kinds of crafts."*
*(Exodus 31:1, 3)*

## SUGGESTED PRAYER

*Dear Lord, you have filled me, _____, with the Spirit of God—with skill, ability, and knowledge. Today I pray that you will help me use my talents and skills to the nth degree! If there is some ability in me that I have not tapped into, please show me, so I can dedicate it to you, along with my other talents and skills. Stretch me, God, into the full measure of who you want me to be. Help me boldly claim my full capacity for your use.*

### So ... What Insight, Prayer, or Action Step Has God Laid on Your Heart Today?

# HOW DO YOU DEFINE SUCCESS?

The world's definition of success is centered around things of this world—things you can earn, buy, demand, manipulate, be, or make. God's view of success is distinctly different: it is that we glorify him by obeying him. Are you ready today to think about prioritizing the two definitions and seeing whether you are more committed to the world's view or to God's? This is a great exercise if you want to finish well the race God has set out for you.

## THE LURE OF SUCCESS

What type of success beckons you? Is it fame, wealth, possessions, power, perfection, or popularity? Is it an impressive job title, getting invited to the right parties, or being a size eight? Is it having a company car and a key to the executive elevator? Is it academic excellence, looking good, meeting deadlines, or having an expense account? Is it being known on a first-name basis at the country club or having a reputation as a big tipper at restaurants? Or, is it more closely aligned with worshiping God with your life? Defining success differently was a radical step for Laura Krauss Calenberg and her husband, who are cofounders of Models for Christ.

## LAURA KRAUSS CALENBERG IS A GREAT ROLE MODEL FOR WOMEN

Laura is a professional model who has traveled the globe on photo shoots, been featured on the runways of top designers, and appeared on the covers of European magazines. She is an author and a sought-after speaker on the topic of inner beauty.

God helped Laura realize that she was in a unique career shared by very few Christians. She seized the opportunity to use the platform for God's glory, and she began to challenge others in her field to do the same. She says that she grows closer to God when she releases his power within her and shares Christ with others.

Laura clearly spells out her definition of success: to bring glory to God. She believes that true success is coming to the place in your life when nothing else will satisfy your longings and desires except Christ. It is when your identity is wrapped up in him and not in yourself.

She says, "A successful person is one who uses the gifts and abilities that God has given her to make a difference. Whatever situation, place, or season she finds herself in, she knows that is the place God has earmarked for her to represent him."

**How Do You Define Success?**

## Zerubbabel Defined Success Well

Zerubbabel, governor of Judah, defined success as being God's servant. Overseer of the temple rebuilding project, he was compared to the Lord's signet ring, which was a symbol of honor, authority, and power. Read Haggai 2:20–23. What public figure today has Zerubbabel's definition of success?

### SCRIPTURE TO PONDER

*Being confident of this, that he who began a good work
in you will carry it on to completion until the day of Christ Jesus.
(Philippians 1:6)*

### SUGGESTED PRAYER

*Dear Christ Jesus, I, _____, am confident of this, that you who began a good work in me will carry it on to completion until the day of your return. I pray that today I will gain more clarity about true success, which is living for you, as you carry out your good work. Let me show up wherever you call me each day and cooperate with you, pointing others to you. Not only do I give you permission to make me successful in your eyes only, I welcome it. The world's success has always left me feeling thirsty for more, but success by your standards will fill me to overflowing.*

## So . . . What Insight, Prayer, or Action Step Has God Laid on Your Heart Today?

# WHO IS YOUR HERO
# OR ROLE MODEL?

Jesus is, of course, our primary hero and role model. Secondary ones might include a biblical character, historical figure, family member, or even a literary character. Who has been a beacon of light, a ray of hope, or an inspiration to you? Who invested him- or herself in your life? Who has filled a critical role for you? We all need someone we can look up to and learn from. Give this some thought today, because such people will nudge you toward God's best for your life.

## WHO'S YOUR INSPIRATION?

Take a moment to think about one of your heroes or role models. Is it a parent, sibling, grandparent, mentor, teacher, pastor, missionary, benefactor, counselor, coach, or doctor? Have you ever cut out a newspaper article on a local hero you admire? Have you learned a great deal by studying the life of the apostle Peter, Eleanor Roosevelt, General Patton, or Don Quixote? Or, have you learned about courage from a terminally ill friend? Karen Braun, director of Mothers Who Care, Canada & International (a ministry of Campus Crusade for Christ), was fortunate as a young girl to have a hero enter into the chaos of her family's life.

## KAREN BRAUN NEEDED A HERO

Disappointments, hurt, ministry challenges, anxiety, and a ten-year struggle with infertility and two failed adoptions have taught Karen to embrace life's lessons through pain to find real peace, freedom, and truth. In addition to her role as director of Mothers Who Care, she is a pastor's wife, mother, daughter, sister, coach, mentor, and friend. She enjoys warm sunny days, color, beauty, reading, and painting.

She has learned that we make our plans, but that God directs our steps. She knows that his way and timing are perfect and that he wastes nothing. She says that she has encountered Truth—Jesus Christ. That relationship has challenged her, changed her, and continues to bring her new life as she surrenders daily to him. Karen's passion is to spark obedience to truth and influence an army to stand for freedom in Christ.

Karen loves to share a story about one of her heroes. He was a man by the name of Wes who, in obedience to the prompting of the Holy Spirit, went to Karen's childhood home to invite her older brothers to Vacation Bible School. Wes arrived on the farm at the exact moment Karen's alcoholic father had a noose around his neck in the barn loft, ready to take his life. Wes was able to share the hope of Jesus Christ with Karen's parents in those next hours, and both souls were saved that day! A direct result of Wes's obedience is that God called Karen and all of her siblings to himself. Three of the four serve in full-time ministry around the world; the entire family has brought hundreds more to a relationship with Christ.

Karen comments: "Real heroes and role models are ordinary people like Wes, who have developed character that has taught them to obey Christ. Their choice to follow God's principles and listen to his Spirit is life-giving to those they are sent to serve."

## Who Is Your Hero or Role Model?

_____

_____

### Daniel Was a Hero

Daniel faced lions rather than bowing to a king whom others adored as a god. Read Daniel 6:1–28. Do you tend to hang around people who are this bold and daring for the Lord? What might such role models inspire you to do?

_____

_____

_____

## SCRIPTURE TO PONDER

*Therefore, since we have a great high priest who has gone through the heavens, Jesus the Son of God, let us hold firmly to the faith we profess. (Hebrews 4:14)*

## SUGGESTED PRAYER

*Dear Lord, since I have you, Jesus the Son of God, a great high priest who has gone through the heavens, let me hold firmly to the faith I, _____, profess. Today I ask you to help me always be receptive to those you send to influence me, those who can guide me to a closer, bolder relationship with you. Reveal to me the name of someone you would like me to learn from during this season of my life. Send me heroes and role models who love you with all their heart. And thank you for those you have already used to shape and mold me.*

**So . . . What Insight, Prayer, or Action Step Has God Laid on Your Heart Today?**

# What Comment or Conversation Has Had a Great Impact on You?

Words can be used to encourage people or destroy them. Conversations can be filled with important instructions or rude admonishments that can change one's life forever. They can bring laughter, memories, or tears. When have words impacted you for good or for bad? Become an expert at blocking out the disrespect, garbage, and insults that miserable souls like to dish out. And, by the way, are you aware of the impact your words have on other people? Do you try to be a good listener when people are speaking to you? Focus today on how God can use conversations to help you fulfill your purposes for him.

## Words Can Be Either Blessings or Curses

Try to remember words that affirmed you or perhaps even some that stung. Did a parent, grandparent, relative, friend, neighbor, teacher, or coworker make a comment to you? Did a boss, store clerk, postal worker, waitress, or psychologist have a conversation with you? Did a playground bully, a dedicated coach, or a guidance counselor have something to say to you?

Denalyn Lucado, who now has a ministry of mercy for single moms, had a series of conversations that turned her life around and healed her aching heart.

## DENALYN LUCADO LISTENED AND LEARNED

Denalyn grew up in a Christian home, became a teacher, and married a Brazil-bound missionary named Max (who is now an author with more than thirty-three million books in print). Her life with him has been a treasure, and being a mom is one of her greatest joys. She says that her ongoing communion with the Lord sustains her, fills her, and humbles her. It has created in her a passion for intercessory praying.

Denalyn freely shares that for years she suffered with depression and anxiety, even though she loved God with all her heart. Her repeated attempts to recover were unsuccessful, until her friend, through tender conversations, helped her understand more about God's grace and mercy. Over time, the Holy Spirit then used the repeatedly kind words of her sister-in-Christ to renew Denalyn's mind and free her from depression, as she more fully understood the assurance and security of her eternal salvation. Denalyn's deeper understanding of God's ways set her free to praise, pray, and play.

After delivering her from depression, the Lord gave Denalyn a ministry of mercy to pray for, encourage, and help single moms in her church. She absolutely loves those women! She says, "Women find intimacy and fellowship in conversation. We encourage or discourage others with our words, so all our communication must flow from a loving heart that is fully dependent on Christ."

## What Comment or Conversation Has Had a Great Impact on You?

### Zacchaeus Was Influenced by a Conversation

Jesus singled out Zacchaeus from a crowd and invited himself to be a houseguest. We don't know the details of their conversation, but we do know that Zacchaeus repented of his sins, promised to make restitution for his wrongdoing, and believed in Jesus. Read Luke 19:1–10. To whom have your words been a blessing lately?

### SCRIPTURE TO PONDER

*May the words of my mouth and the meditation of my heart be pleasing in your sight, O LORD, my Rock and my Redeemer. (Psalm 19:14)*

### SUGGESTED PRAYER

*O Lord, my Rock and my Redeemer, may the words of my mouth and the meditation of my heart be pleasing in your sight. Today I, _____, ask you to help me become acutely aware of how my comments and conversations positively or negatively affect others, how they build or destroy. Guide my conversations, so that through my words, you will fill others with hope and courage. And, if I need to speak a hard truth, let me do so from a loving heart filled to overflowing with your grace. Let me truly be the mouthpiece of your Holy Spirit when I speak and his ears when I listen.*

## So . . . What Insight, Prayer, or Action Step Has God Laid on Your Heart Today?

# WHAT ARE TWO OF YOUR BEST PERSONAL QUALITIES?

Nobody likes to brag, so let me make this question easy on you by explaining that it is important for you to know what your best qualities are, so you can maximize them for God's work. In fact, today is really all about identifying how Christ's character traits shine through your personality. Let your answer give you insight about how you can better serve the Lord in your home, workplace, and community. It's okay to "phone a friend" to get your final answer! Then, let God have the best part of you to use as he chooses.

## PUT YOUR BEST FOOT FORWARD

What's most lovable or admirable about you? Is it your loyalty, responsibility, generosity, focus, authenticity, kindness, or patience? Does God smile at your forgiving, gentle, and encouraging nature; your prayerfulness; your surrendered heart; or your humorous antics? Do others notice your humility, tactfulness, risk-taking, creativity, passion, or perseverance? Is your best quality your respectfulness, reliability, empathy, wisdom, calmness, or ability to laugh at yourself? Or is God most pleased with your honesty, fairness, purity, or gratitude? Sue Semrau, women's head basketball coach at Florida State University, asked her friends to help her answer today's question.

## SUE SEMRAU GETS RAVE REVIEWS

As the women's basketball coach, Sue engineered a turn-around of the Seminole program at Florida State. After only her fourth season, she was named Atlantic Coast Conference Coach of the Year.

Sue feels that her godly platform of athletics is indeed an exciting one. She gets to use some of her favorite tools—a leather ball and a hardwood court—as her opportunity to reflect Christ and share the gospel. She resonates with the words of Francis of Assisi who urged believers to "preach the gospel always, and when necessary, use words."

Colleagues praise Sue's lifestyle of integrity, saying that she sets high standards and refuses to compromise her character in any situation. In addition, Sue's friends feel that she has a genuine compassion for people that goes beyond logic to meet needs. She says, "When I'm conscious of who I'm representing, I best reflect that which Christ himself has cultivated in me. I strive to be the same person privately and publicly."

**What Are Two of Your Best Personal Qualities?**

### Abigail Had Great Personal Qualities

Abigail had incredible courage and wisdom in the face of imminent danger. Read 1 Samuel 25:1–44. What two qualities do you wish you had? Will you ask God to help you develop them?

## SCRIPTURE TO PONDER

*But just as he who called you is holy, so be holy in all you do.*
*(1 Peter 1:15)*

## SUGGESTED PRAYER

*Dear Lord, just as you who called me are holy, so help me, _____, to be holy in all I do. Today I thank you for my best qualities, and I ask that you will grow me in character and help me be more _____ [fill in a personal quality here]. Remind me to be continually aware of you, the one I am representing.*

## So . . . What Insight, Prayer, or Action Step Has God Laid on Your Heart Today?

# How Do You
# Self-Sabotage?

Are you a saboteur? Self-sabotage means that you consciously or subconsciously obstruct your own productivity in order to underhandedly defeat a worthwhile endeavor. It's how you ensure that you will not be expected to complete God's plan for your life. Most women are not even aware that they are, at least occasionally, sabotaging their success.

## What Is Your Most Devious Method
## of Sabotaging God's Plan for Your Life?

Could this be your story? You don't exercise, thus causing health issues; you remain addicted to sugar and keep yourself tired and irritable; you are rash and impulsive, which results in poor, irreversible decisions. Or is this more like you? You compare yourself to others and end up feeling inadequate; you aim for perfection, which inevitably leads to failure; you allow your temper to rage out of control, producing guilt and shame. What about harboring a sense of entitlement, which fills you with pride? Do you stay up too late and act like a grouch the next day? Do you overindulge at meals and then get severely depressed about your weight gain? Do you choose to be disorganized and therefore wreak havoc in your life? Kay Warren, a passionate advocate for those around the world infected/affected by HIV/AIDS, has become very aware of her efforts to self-sabotage.

## KAY WARREN KNOWS WHAT SHE'S DOING

Kay is a mother of three, grandmother of one, an international speaker, coauthor of *Foundations: 11 Core Truths to Build Your Life On*, and breast cancer survivor. She is the wife of Rick, who is the founding pastor of Saddleback Church and author of *The Purpose-Driven Life*.

Kay has the rich heritage of growing up in a pastor's home, where she learned from an early age to love the Lord deeply and to live for his purposes. She encourages women not to waste their emotional and spiritual energy wishing God had made them differently, but to recognize that he chooses and uses ordinary people in extraordinary ways!

Kay has devised a great method of self-sabotage. She confesses that she sometimes would rather be right than relational, because being right inflates her self-worth. Because of her highly defined sense of justice, she admits that she can be too intent on fending off challenges in a conflict, rather than yielding on unimportant issues. This, of course, leads to hurt feelings, and it tears down relationships rather than building them. As closeness is sacrificed, her ability to be effective is sabotaged.

She says, "We women are experts at incapacitating ourselves relationally, mentally, emotionally, spiritually, and financially. We plan our own demise; nobody has to do it for us! And, foolish as it sounds, we often blame God for the problems we cause in our lives."

### How Do You Self-Sabotage?

### A Criminal Probably Sabotaged His Last Chance to Get into Heaven

Out of anger and arrogance, one of the criminals being crucified with Jesus hurled insults at him and, as far as we know, was not invited to enter eternal paradise. Read about this ultimate example of self-sabotage in Luke 23:39–43. In what way have you noticed someone sabotaging his or her chances at success?

## SCRIPTURE TO PONDER

*Let us examine our ways and test them, and let us return to the LORD. (Lamentations 3:40)*

## SUGGESTED PRAYER

*Dear Lord, let me, _____, examine my ways today and test them. I return to you and ask for your protection, that I will not try to derail myself from accomplishing my best for you. I ask specifically that you will keep me from my most ingenious method of self-sabotage. Give me the wisdom to stop it!*

**So . . . What Insight, Prayer, or Action Step Has God Laid on Your Heart Today?**

# WHAT'S RIGHT AND WHAT'S WRONG IN YOUR LIFE?

We all have dozens of things right and wrong in our lives. What one thing is going well for you today, and what one thing is a burden on your heart? It's important to get in the habit of clarifying the truth about your life, so you will learn to live more often in gratitude, as well as create the right solutions and support systems, when needed. In fact, learning to make realistic appraisals and recommendations for improvements is a valuable skill that will come in handy for completing God's plan for your life.

## IS IT RIGHT OR IS IT WRONG?

Things fluctuate between right and wrong on a regular basis, so for today, it's okay to take a general approach to these two questions, cleverly disguised as one! How are your career, ministry, marriage, savings account, transportation, life purpose, and travel schedule? How are you doing with your in-laws, neighbor's pets, insurance rates, budget, salary, or interest rates? What about your perception of God and your trust in his love for you? How are your relationships, your random acts of kindness, or your hopes for a bright future? Anything going on with your health, spiritual growth, or child care arrangements? Dr. RoseAnne Coleman, founder of RoseAnne Coleman Ministries, loves honest appraisals.

## ROSEANNE COLEMAN TELLS IT LIKE IT IS

RoseAnne's not-for-profit organization has been providing transitional crisis housing for women and their children since 1994. Her latest project is a property called Rose Hill, where RoseAnne hopes women soon can come to be quiet and listen to the Lord, as they sit on the porch swing or help tend the flowers.

RoseAnne loves God's Word and telling others what she has found in it. For eighteen years, she has taught the Bible to groups, locally and around the world. She tries to live in the moment-by-moment reality of God's presence, knowing for a fact that the Lord cares about everything and everyone she meets. RoseAnne wishes she had amazing abilities, physical beauty, and a wonderful personality to lead others to the Lord, but instead she offers her honesty about her brokenness and struggles. Her joy is to show the Lord's incredible love, mercy, and presence to earthbound stumblers like herself.

What's right and what's wrong for RoseAnne? She admits that she is creative (not administrative); about a B+ on the personality scale; unable to remember where she just put her pen; and certain that her disorganized home will *not* be featured in *Real Simple* magazine. She is global in processing information and visual in learning. She says that, although she is not the poster child for motivational speakers or for the perfect Christian woman, she is beginning to realize how much God loves her—and is humbled daily at his attention to her. It is in that astonished wonder that she tries to live.

RoseAnne says, "For years I had *faith* that God would provide my external needs but didn't *trust* him to heal the dark chaos of my heart. My mother, Melrose, helped with my problems until she died in 1999. Not long ago when I was struggling to trust God with a paralyzing weakness, I thought I heard Momma's sweet voice in my head. Although afraid I had had a sunstroke, I asked her, 'What have you learned in heaven?' Maybe God spoke his truth in the voice I trusted the most, for the words stunned and changed me forever: 'He is more faithful than you could imagine. You can trust him.' So daily I am trying to trust him to heal and transform what is wrong and broken in my life, and to thank him for what is right and holy."

**What's Right in Your Life?**

**What's Wrong in Your Life?**

### The Lame Man Had Something Wrong and Something Right in His Life

The lame man couldn't get into the pool to be healed when the waters stirred. However, the wonderful conclusion to his story has been told for centuries, giving the hope of Jesus' miraculous, albeit delayed, intervention to millions who think they have no hope. Read John 5:1–15. Have you or a friend ever thanked God for a "righted" wrong?

## SCRIPTURE TO PONDER

*However many years a man may live, let him enjoy them all.*
*But let him remember the days of darkness, for they will be many.*
*(Ecclesiastes 11:8)*

## SUGGESTED PRAYER

*Dear Lord, however many years I, _____, may live, let*
*me enjoy them all. But let me never forget the days of darkness*
*that come because of our fallen world, for they will be many.*
*I know that remembering the good and the bad, the right and*
*the wrong in my life, will give me a broader perspective for*
*gratitude and problem solving. I ask you to help me today*
*to be more honest about what is right and wrong in my life.*
*Lead me away from confusion and denial. Lead me into your*
*truth and clarity, so that I will become more fruitful for you.*

**So . . . What Insight, Prayer, or Action Step**
**Has God Laid on Your Heart Today?**

# What Was a Turning Point in Your Life?

A turning point in your life can be a minor incident, a major event, or a sudden realization which causes you to change, either for the good or bad, the course you are on. It is a time during which you take stock of your situation and then take action. It can be a dramatic wake-up call to stop doing something, or it can be a simple, conversational affirmation that makes you finally pay attention to one of your life dreams. What in your life has caused you to turn from Plan A to Plan B? And what was the result of that change in direction? God wants to be intimately involved in all the turning points of your life. He knows there is much at stake for his kingdom-building plans, and he wants to see you through!

## Did You Change Your Course?

A turning point in your life could have been an illness, accident, graduation, household move, betrayal, major disappointment, or the realization that you were "bored out of your mind." It could have been a joyful conversion to Christianity or complete surrender to Christ as Lord. It might have been an inheritance that dramatically improved your lot in life or unleashed sin in your life. It could have been a baby's birth or the death of a loved one. It could have been a job lay-off or a crumbled marriage. Janet Congo, cofounder (with her husband) of LifeMates, was thrown a curve ball that caused her to head in a new, unexpected direction.

## JANET CONGO'S LIFE TOOK AN UNEXPECTED TURN

Janet is a wife, mother of two adult children, marriage and family therapist, life coach, university instructor, nationally known speaker, and author of eleven books on topics including marriage, stress, love, and self-confidence. Her ministry, LifeMates, strengthens Christian marriages through regular Date Nite events in churches around the United States.

Janet describes herself as having been "set free by Jesus Christ's sacrifice, empowered by his Holy Spirit, and deeply influenced by his Word." She says that, as a result, "she exists to love consistently, learn continually, live courageously, and leave a legacy with God's principles as her guide." She seeks to empower, encourage, and inspire women to love God, to be loved by God, to discover who he meant them to be, and to infuse their marriages with that divine love.

A major turning point in Janet's life came when the United States Immigration Department informed her that, even though she had been hired by a California college as an instructor, she could not teach because she was Canadian and would be taking a job away from an American. She remembers well the shock of hearing that news and having to restructure her career. So, she purposefully and tenaciously changed gears, began writing books, and is thrilled with the alternate path that God made available to her!

Janet believes that "turning points occur when our plans and reality collide. Disappointments, failures, tragedies, and dead ends all provide an opportunity to ask 'Why?' and become a victim or to ask 'What next?' and cooperate with God about the next phase of our life!"

## What Was a Turning Point in Your Life?

## Saul Had a Major Turning Point

Saul, a persecutor of Christians whose name was later changed to Paul, experienced a 180-degree turnaround in his life when he encountered Jesus on the road to Damascus. Read Acts 9:1–22. Have you allowed your turning points to draw you closer to God or to push you farther from him?

## SCRIPTURE TO PONDER

*Show me the way I should go, for to you I lift up my soul.*
*(Psalm 143:8)*

## Suggested Prayer

*Dear Lord, show me, _____, the way I should go today, for to you I lift up my soul. I pray that I will continue to learn from my past experiences and decisions, letting you turn my life around 180 degrees, if necessary. I thank you in advance for any turning points I have yet to face that will ultimately bring me closer to you. Guide me to those moments that will take my breath away in gratitude for your direction in my life.*

**So . . . What Insight, Prayer, or Action Step Has God Laid on Your Heart Today?**

# WHAT ROADBLOCKS HAVE YOU ENCOUNTERED IN YOUR LIFE?

Do you feel as if you face roadblocks everywhere you turn in your family life, ministry, or career? Roadblocks to your dreams, intimacy, or continuing education? What's Murphy's Law? *If anything can go wrong, it will.* What a truism! So, what roadblocks have you had to outmaneuver on life's pathway? Are you stalled by the same one each time or do new ones keep taking you by surprise? Regardless of whether you've encountered one or more roadblocks, it is important to establish some best practices for navigating through. How you deal with the delays and difficulties you face today will affect whether you are able to complete God's plan for your life.

## ROADBLOCKS GALORE

Have you ever been stopped dead in your tracks by one of these persistent headaches: insufficient knowledge, a critical spirit, laziness, shifting agendas, or not being connected with the right people? Has your biggest roadblock been not owning land to build on, not knowing how to write a grant, overcommitment, or personal pride? Has it been a lack of faith or financing? Was it a personal inhibition, an illness, exhaustion, people politics, or procrastination? Is it currently the green-eyed monster of jealousy, or is it, perhaps, a standing invitation to a self-pity party that you simply can never resist? Ann Platz, an interior designer for twenty-eight years, made an executive decision not to let a particular roadblock stop her any longer.

## ANN PLATZ NOW TAKES FULL ADVANTAGE OF ROADBLOCKS

Ann is an author of eleven books on topics such as reclaiming your dreams and the pleasure of having company. She is also a book illustrator and a speaker who plants hope, imparts courage, and helps women invite beauty and love into their hearts. She is dedicated to transformation, especially in herself! Ann loves growing in her faith and opening her home to others to experience grace-filled moments of hospitality.

Ann's passion is mentoring women. She thinks of herself as a heart-opener, that is, one who is privileged to be God's tool for opening the hearts of women. In this role, she helps them see God's intended sphere of influence for them on earth. She cherishes the opportunities that she has to watch women become vessels of grace, those whom God uses to impact his world. She encourages women and cheers them on toward their purposes and destinies. She has even written a book on the topic, *Guardians of the Gate: Enriching Your Life through Spiritual Mentoring*.

Ann's biggest roadblock was a control issue that centered around abrupt changes. When a scheduled meeting was canceled at the last minute, she would become very agitated and irritated. She did not like feeling that way, because she did not like losing the peace of the Lord. As she began to question her reaction to having her schedule disrupted, it became apparent that she had a choice to make about her negative attitude. Eventually, Ann decided to use delays as an opportunity to trust the Lord with her time. She now chooses to let the Lord order her steps, anticipating that he will use her rescheduled times for his plan. Now these roadblocks have become times of refreshment and are actually joyful for her!

She says, "I finally figured out that roadblocks are often God's test of our character; other times they are just life or the enemy's plan to use discouragement to halt our journey of spiritual growth. I am convinced that obstacles can become incredible doors of opportunities to those who choose to pray their way through them."

## What Roadblocks Have You Encountered in Your Career, Ministry, or Family Life?

### Ruth Had a Roadblock

When Ruth's husband died, she had to decide whether to react with a positive or negative spirit. Read Ruth 1:1–18. If you had been Ruth, how would you have dealt with this roadblock? (My heart goes out to you, if you have been Ruth.)

## SCRIPTURE TO PONDER

*"I [Jesus] have told you these things, so that in me you may have peace. In this world you will have trouble. But take heart! I have overcome the world." (John 16:33)*

## SUGGESTED PRAYER

*Dear Lord Jesus, you have told me, _____, about your relationship with God your Father and about his love for me, so that in you, I may have peace. I know that in this world I will have trouble, but I take heart because you have overcome the world. I pray today that you, as my King, will remove roadblocks for me or help me mature spiritually as I hurdle them. I pray, too, that you will reveal to me when you are putting up a barricade to stop me versus when you are inviting me to climb over it with you. If I hear you calling me, please give me a spirit of fearlessness when it comes to overcoming obstacles.*

## So . . . What Insight, Prayer, or Action Step Has God Laid on Your Heart Today?

# What Are Your Hobbies?

God made you to be attracted to certain topics, and he may even have used your family or environment to assist you in acquiring some of your interests. A hobby might relax you, rejuvenate your spirit, or completely invigorate you. It might keep you in good physical shape, or it may be good mental conditioning for you. It may simply be fun—causing you to be playful—or it may earn you a profit from time to time. No matter what your hobby does for *you*, why not consider letting God have it to bless his work on earth? His creativity at weaving the gist of your hobby into your church ministry or life mission will amaze you.

## What Makes Your Heart Sing?

What sets you free from the cares and worries of this world? Is it snowboarding, researching, or traveling the world? Is it dog grooming, scrapbooking, sculpting, or painting? What do you get lost in for hours? Is it creating miniature Christmas villages, complete with model trains? Is it judging annual flower competitions or umpiring Little League games? Is it hiking, reading mysteries, or collecting thimbles or stuffed bears? It might be training horses, mountain biking, playing chess, or hunting for bargain antiques. Pay attention to the components of your hobby, to see if any part of it can be used to serve God and others. For example, could you sing jazz concerts at a senior center? Could you prepare a gourmet meal for your pastor's family? Ronda Rich, one of America's first female sportswriters, loves to watch God use her refreshing hobby.

## RONDA RICH THANKS GOD FOR HER HOBBY

Ronda is an award-winning journalist and bestselling author of *What Southern Women Know* and *My Life in the Pits: Living and Learning on the NASCAR Winston Cup Circuit.* Raised a preacher's child, she is thrilled to actually have been baptized in a river! She enjoys sharing God's love and blessings with secular audiences through writing and speaking about life lessons she has learned.

Ronda's hobby is to collect memories about unique experiences with her friends. She weaves her reflections into great stories to tell around the dinner table and some even make it into her writing. She says, "God knows that we are driven by our passions, because he created us to be eager to do what we enjoy. The desires of our heart are quite simply God's way of giving us a compass for the paths he wants us to take. For that, I am so grateful."

**What Are Your Hobbies?**

_____

_____

### Dorcas Had a Hobby

Dorcas was a seamstress who discovered that her hobby had become a ministry when she sewed clothes to help the poor and the widows of her town. She was dearly loved for her acts of kindness. Read Acts 9:36–42. Can you imagine one of your hobbies paying such spiritual dividends?

_____

_____

## SCRIPTURE TO PONDER

*Delight yourself in the LORD and he will give you the desires of your heart. (Psalm 37:4)*

## SUGGESTED PRAYER

*Dear Lord, I, _____, find delight in knowing you, and I thank you for your promise to give me the desires of my heart. Today I pray that my hobbies will not only give me joy in life but, much more importantly, that they will be a compass for the path you would like me to take. I ask you to turn an enjoyable hobby of mine into a personal contribution, a real opportunity to serve those you want me to serve.*

## So . . . What Insight, Prayer, or Action Step Has God Laid on Your Heart Today?

# WHO IS IN
# YOUR NETWORK?

Are you surrounded by groups of people at home, church, school, or work who say to you such things as: "We're all in this together"; "How can we help you today?"; "If you're hurting, we're hurting"? This is what God had in mind: that we would all watch out for one another. He's not much interested in excuses: "I'm an introvert," "I'm too busy to be in a small group at church," or "I've *tried* to meet my neighbors!" Let Scripture talk to you today about how living life in community with others can help you accomplish your godly life purposes.

## PROFESSIONAL, MINISTERIAL, OR EMOTIONAL NETWORKS THAT REALLY WORK

If you've ever been in a career- or ministry-focused network, you know that those relationships are extremely valuable. You currently may be in a season-of-life group such as MOPS (Mothers of Preschoolers), or you may be staying in touch with friends you made at a writers' conference. Perhaps you meet with a Christian counselor for marital support. Or maybe you are in a weekly class at church, a carpool, a loving family, or a

babysitting co-op. See how Andria Hall, founder of SpeakEasy
M.E.D.I.A., counts on her support system.

## ANDRIA HALL COLLECTS FRIENDS

Andria is a veteran broadcast journalist, former weekend
anchor for the CNN/USA cable network, author, wife, and
mother of three children. After achieving worldly success, she
discovered that it all rings hollow without an authentic and intimate relationship with Jesus Christ. Andria now dedicates her
life to the acronym for which her media and public presentation
company, SpeakEasy M.E.D.I.A., stands: to *Minister, Edify,
and Divinely Inspire All . . .* to the glory of God. She encourages others to believe that they can do God's will *and* do it well.

Andria says that she craves a closer connection to God. She
firmly believes that her top priority is to seek what's important
to him. She says that all the other stuff—professional connec-
tions, monetary gain, business growth, and so on—has developed when she has stayed focused on God's plan, not her own.
Regardless of the stuff, she's all his! Andria believes that true
success is attainable only by yielding to the transforming power
of Jesus Christ. She is called to help others work purposefully
for God and to realize that the pursuit of excellence is not
optional.

Andria counts herself blessed because God has placed in her
life a network of close friends, reliable professional contacts,
and caring brothers and sisters in Christ, who have been
ordained by God to "do life" with her. To receive the gift of
loving support, she focuses on offering the same. She thinks of
people as souls first and contacts last.

She sums up: "If God has allowed someone to enter my life—even if that person's intentions are not godly, it is for a reason. I ask the Holy Spirit to help me figure out if a person is in my life to learn from, fellowship with, or minister to. After all, he is the expert on how to develop meaningful relationships, which is the basic principle of networking."

## Who Is in Your Professional, Ministerial, or Emotional Network?


### Jesus Had a Ministerial Network of Friends

Jesus called the twelve apostles to help him with his work on earth. Eleven of them modeled the value of relationships. Three became Christ's best friends. Read Matthew 10:1–8. What efforts have you made to be surrounded by best friends?


## SCRIPTURE TO PONDER

*By yourself you're unprotected. With a friend you can face the worst. Can you round up a third? A three-stranded rope isn't easily snapped. (Ecclesiastes 4:12, MSG)*

## Suggested Prayer

*Dear Lord, by myself I, _____, am unprotected. With a friend, I can face the worst. Can you help me round up a third? A three-stranded rope isn't easily snapped. Today I pray that I will be surrounded by godly networks. Open doors for me to meet just the right people at just the right time, who will lovingly support your will for my life. Bring lots of us together to humbly serve you and each other.*

**So . . . What Insight, Prayer, or Action Step Has God Laid on Your Heart Today?**

# WHAT WERE YOU BORN TO TELL THE WORLD?

God has gifted you with a life message to share with the world. That message or idea is what he wants you to communicate to others. Being chosen as one of God's spokespersons is both an important responsibility and an awesome privilege. Some women run from the task; others experiment with it for only a brief period of time; and some fully embrace it. Just remember that a message is not a message until it is delivered! It is your choice today to decide how you will respond to God's invitation to carry his message to his world. It might be interesting for you to take note of what message your friends like to share with others for God! Uncovering their life messages will definitely give you a clue about God's plan for their lives and why you like them so much. Perhaps their life message challenges you or helps you refocus.

## GOD-GIVEN PROCLAMATIONS

Have you noticed that the same encouraging comment comes spilling out of your heart and mouth all the time? For example, *Hope against all odds.* Or, *Jesus loves you.* Do you sometimes feel like a preacher when you say to someone: *Serve as if you are serving Jesus.* Or, *you will find freedom in Christ.* What Christlike theme ranks at the top of your list? *Love one another.* Or, *surrender to Jesus Christ today.* What do you wish you could shout from the mountaintop? *Forgive one another.* Or, *protect unborn babies.* Diane Dunne, street preacher to New York City's homeless, loves being a bold and practical messenger for God.

## DIANE DUNNE SPEAKS OUT

Diane experienced success working her way up the corporate ladder at Chanel, a prestigious cosmetics company. Later, after her conversion to Christ, she went to work in a Christian bookstore. Eventually, she teamed up with Teen Challenge and began working with youth in street evangelism. In 1987, she founded Hope for the Future Ministries, where she pastors the Church Without Walls on the streets of New York City's Lower East Side. Diane has served as an evangelist for the past twenty-one years. She believes that a building does not make a church, but that *we* are the universal church!

Diane loves to minister to and feed the poor and homeless, especially those who are elderly. Her message: *God does not discriminate. Regardless of race, socioeconomic status, age, education, denomination, or personal plans, he will use the heart that is willing to serve him.* Diane's earnest conviction is to tell others to live out their passion and to reach their full potential in Christ.

She says, "Our heavenly Father is constantly thinking about us and desires us to have a spiritually intimate relationship with him. He wants us to transform an uncaring and self-serving society into a radical church that seeks opportunities outside the proverbial box—in its service for him. Whatever message he gave you to share, why not start sharing it now with passion? You will be blessed."

## What Were You Born to Tell the World?

## John the Baptist Had a Life Message from God

John the Baptist was sent to prepare the way for the Lord. His life message: "Repent, for the kingdom of heaven is near." Read Matthew 3:1–12. How would you like to have been assigned John's message and place in history?

## SCRIPTURE TO PONDER

*However, I consider my life worth nothing to me,*
*if only I may finish the race and complete the task the Lord Jesus*
*has given me—the task of testifying to the gospel of God's grace.*
*(Acts 20:24)*

## Suggested Prayer

*Dear Lord Jesus, I, _____, consider my life worth nothing to me, if only I may finish the race and complete the task you have given me—the task of testifying to the gospel of God's grace. Today I seek to know and deliver the message that I was sent into the world to carry. What an awesome privilege to be a trusted messenger.*

**So . . . What Insight, Prayer, or Action Step Has God Laid on Your Heart Today?**

# How Is God Developing Your Character?

Do you know how a pearl develops? It happens when a foreign substance slips into an oyster between its mantle and shell. This irritates the oyster, much like a splinter might bother you. The oyster reacts to cover up and protect itself from the irritant with layers of a natural substance, eventually forming a pearl.

God has a similar process for developing character. You sometimes experience irritants through physical and emotional pain, or through trials, temptations, or delays. When you react in a godly way to such mild or severe *irritants*, an extraordinary character is formed in you. You may feel as though God has been using heavenly sandpaper, instead, to shape your character! With either method, he has probably been taking full advantage of life's rigorous and varied situations to help you grow spiritually, because good character is critical to fulfilling his plan for your life.

## God Is an Expert At Shaping Character

Have you been dealing with particularly difficult people lately? If so, perhaps you are learning about the importance of patience. Is God asking you to tithe to teach you obedience, commitment, and generosity? Has he allowed you to remain in a situation in which you have said, "My back is against the wall," so you would learn to trust him? Has an unfair decision taught you about wisdom and honesty? Has suffering invited humility along? Eva Marie Everson, who often speaks on behalf of the National Coalition for the Protection of Children and Families, has been an eyewitness to God's powerful transformation of her character, even when she dragged her heels along the way!

## Eva Marie Everson Is a Work-In-Progress

Eva Marie is an award-winning author of fiction and non-fiction books, a nationally recognized speaker, and a former teacher of Old Testament at her church. She often uses drama in her messages to relate the truth. Research for her *Shadows* trilogy led her to begin educating parents about the dangers of pornography in their children's lives.

Though Eva Marie has loved the Lord passionately her entire life, she says that she was surprised that her trip to Israel in 2002 (as a journalist) changed her spiritually. From that time on, having seen and touched the places where the story of Christ unfolded, she began seeking to know more about the heart of God. Eva Marie began to see the Bible as a powerful report of what truly happened to real people as ordinary as herself.

Through the reading and writing of books, God is teaching Eva Marie about his grace and mercy, two gifts she confesses she has withheld from others for years. Through relationships, both the ones that mutually encourage and the ones that take unending effort, God is opening her heart to the pain and hardships of others. She says that she realizes more and more that "there but by the grace of God go I." This compassion now allows her to touch people's lives in ways she never before thought she could.

Eva Marie reflects on a truth she has learned about how God works: "Every day I feel a little more of me slipping away and a little more of God being replaced there. While I truly desire this, still I find myself holding on to self. In each area of my life, God is good enough to allow me to hold on, until I'm miserable enough to let go on my own."

## How Is God Developing Your Character?

## Philip Needed His Character Developed

Philip, one of the twelve apostles, was sometimes a skeptic who could not express a firm belief about the power of Jesus. So, Jesus tested him to help develop him as a man of faith and conviction. Read John 6:5–12. If you could tell God how you would like your next character trait developed, what process would you suggest he use?

## SCRIPTURE TO PONDER

*You also, like living stones, are being built into a spiritual house
to be a holy priesthood, offering spiritual sacrifices acceptable
to God through Jesus Christ. (1 Peter 2:5)*

## SUGGESTED PRAYER

*Dear Lord God, like a living stone, I, _____, am being
built into a spiritual house to be a holy priest, offering spiritual
sacrifices acceptable to you through Jesus Christ. Today I pray
that you will continue to shape me into the woman you want
me to be. Help me, as one who desperately needs your work
in my life. I give you permission to mold me into the woman
you already see me as. But please, walk with me every step
of the way!*

### So . . . What Insight, Prayer, or Action Step Has God Laid on Your Heart Today?

# WHAT HAS BEEN YOUR FAVORITE JOB, MINISTRY, OR COMMUNITY VOLUNTEER OPPORTUNITY?

Once your heart has raced with excitement during a career assignment, church ministry activity, or community role, you will probably crave that exhilarating feeling again. What great memory comes to mind about a paid or volunteer position in which you had the time of your life? Did it make you smile and sigh and feel grateful to be involved? Do you feel that God's hand was in that situation? Do you understand that he delights in giving you tasks he designed you to love?

## DOES LIFE GET ANY BETTER THAN THIS?

What career delights your soul and allows you to be a witness for Jesus in the marketplace? Is it being a newspaper reporter, forensic scientist, mother, electrician, beautician, financial advisor, or flight attendant? Do you most enjoy consulting, entrepreneuring, or working at a public relations firm? What church ministry do you look forward to on a regular basis? Is it being a church office volunteer, recycling cans to pay for Bibles, directing the choir, designing a ministry website, supervising lay counselors, or mentoring young girls? Is it being a greeter at worship services, teaching a Bible class, or doing telephone evangelism? What community volunteer task is invigorating for you and gives you a chance at friendship evangelism? Do you love to organize the annual pancake breakfast for your local Kiwanis Club, work at a pet rescue clinic, care for elderly shut-ins, grocery shop for a women's shelter, serve on a board of trustees, or be a Cub Scout master? It could be that nothing makes you happier than directing plays at your community theater, being on-call for the Red Cross disaster relief team, or being a fundraiser for the Leukemia Society. Barbara Smith, author of *Cooking with Smitty's Mom*, has pinpointed her favorite service opportunities.

## BARBARA SMITH HAS A SERVANT'S HEART

Barbara is the mother of recording artist Michael W. Smith. She was a church secretary for twenty-seven years and owned a catering business; now she enjoys occasional speaking engagements. She prays to become more Christlike in her actions toward others. She also prays often for wisdom, because she believes Proverbs 24:3: "By wisdom a house is built, and through understanding it is established."

Because Barbara's childhood was difficult, she knows that her passion for making family a priority is her special gift from God. Barbara's favorite job has always been as a mom. She loves to provide a God-centered, spiritual place where her family *belongs*. And, more recently, she has enjoyed encouraging young mothers within and outside her church. She coaches them to plan daily for quality, family time together and to prayerfully and constantly seek God's counsel for the choices they make as a family. Barbara is a servant whenever God opens a door. She uses her love of food preparation as a ministry to sick and bereaved members of her church and neighborhood, and she thoroughly enjoys feeding the homeless through a program called Room at the Inn.

She comments: "It boggles my mind that the Creator of the universe would worry about details, like whether or not I enjoy my assignments from him. Frankly, though, I love this feeling of being spoiled by my heavenly Father to the point of being allowed to serve in my element! He may soon need me to serve elsewhere, outside my area of passion, but for now, I certainly consider it a treat to be doing what I love doing."

### What Has Been Your Favorite Job, Ministry, or Community Volunteer Opportunity?

### Deborah Had a Favorite Job

Deborah, the only known female judge of Israel, sang the celebratory Song of Deborah recorded in Judges 5:1–31. That festivity had to be a career highlight for her because, along with Barak and his army, she was able to stop the king of Canaan's twenty-year reign of terror on their land. Read her story in Judges 4:1–23. Who do you know who has had the opportunity, like Deborah, to do something heart-pounding or life-giving at home, work, church, or in his or her community? What was it?

## SCRIPTURE TO PONDER

*LORD, you have assigned me my portion and my cup;*
*you have made my lot secure. The boundary lines have fallen*
*for me in pleasant places; surely I have a delightful inheritance.*
*(Psalm 16:5-6)*

## SUGGESTED PRAYER

*Dear Lord, you have assigned me, _____, my portion*
*and my cup; you have made my lot secure. The boundary lines*
*have fallen for me in pleasant places; surely I have a delightful*
*inheritance. Today I thank you for the rich and fulfilling*
*experiences you have given me or have reserved especially for*
*me in the future. Whether in a paid career, an unsalaried*
*household management position, a church ministry position,*
*or a community volunteer opportunity, I want to follow in*
*your footsteps, representing your goodness to others. I pray for*
*a willingness to serve humbly, not wanting to draw attention*
*to myself. Let me be useful to you.*

### So . . . What Insight, Prayer, or Action Step Has God Laid on Your Heart Today?

# IN WHAT SITUATION WAS GOD'S POWER EVIDENT TO YOU?

Nothing is impossible for God. He laid the foundation of the world! When have you witnessed his power? Have you seen him walking on water to get to you when you were in distress? Has he calmed a storm or multiplied loaves for you? He has promised to see you through every circumstance of life. Take time today to recall a situation in which his power was evident to you. Remembering the miracles in your life will help you live with gratitude. It will ready your heart to serve more faithfully the Almighty God who has important assignments lined up for you.

## NOTHING COMPARES TO THE POWER OF GOD

God formed the mountains, hung the stars, and churned up the seas. He answers prayers, grants mercy, and gives hope. What aspect of God's power has most astounded you? Is it his wisdom, healing touch, or unforeseen solutions? Is it peace amidst turmoil that he gives you or the renewal of your strength? Is it the fact that he has rescued you at the last hour? Did he help you through exams, childbirth, illness, or the death of a dear friend? Did he stay by you on a difficult trip overseas, your first day on a new job, or an escrow closing? Did he see you through a natural disaster or some other tragedy? Did he resurrect a relationship or give you ingenuity to complete a project beyond your highest expectations? Have you witnessed his power in the changed life of a friend or family member? Fern Nichols, founder of Moms In Touch International (MITI), is in awe of our all-powerful God who has proven time and time again that he cares about her.

## FERN NICHOLS HUMBLY EXPECTS GOD TO SHOW UP

For the first fifteen years of Fern's marriage, she and her husband served at Athletes in Action, an arm of Campus Crusade for Christ. Later, she founded MITI, a worldwide ministry of praying moms who gather together locally once a week to pray for their children and their children's schools. Her favorite roles, though, are as a wife, mother, and grandma.

Fern is grateful for her Christian heritage and for a mom who taught her about prayer and the infallibility of God's Word. During her college years, she had a spiritual growth spurt and became involved in InterVarsity Christian Fellowship/USA, an evangelical campus ministry. She has developed a deep love for the church, as the body of Christ.

As Fern sent her two oldest sons off to junior high school, she found herself passionately praying for them. She knew that her greatest weapon to protect them from the pressures they would be facing was prayer. The burden was so great that she knew she could not bear it alone. She asked God for another mother who felt the same burden and who would pray every week for their kids and the local school. One mom came, then another, and another. Twenty years later, more than 150,000 women are praying for children and schools worldwide. Fern now loves teaching about prayer, and she is humbled that God chose her to raise this prayer banner a little higher.

Fern notes that she experiences God's sustaining power when she speaks publicly. She says that, as she prepares a talk—with a cramped scheduled, little rest, and many demands—she realizes that her source of power is in knowing her God and experiencing his goodness in her circumstances. She says, "He proves himself always to be faithful and gives me peace with his promise that when I open my mouth, he will fill it and will take me from strength to strength."

Fern purposefully seeks his power in her life through prayer and his Word. One of her favorite passages of Scripture that she prays for herself, husband, children, and Moms In Touch is "that you will be strengthened with his glorious power so that you will have all the patience and endurance you need" (Colossians 1:11, NLT).

### In What Situation Was God's Power Evident to You?

### Lazarus Saw God's Power

Lazarus saw the power of Jesus Christ, as Jesus called on God his Father, to raise Lazarus from the dead. Read John

11:1–44. Perhaps you need something raised from the dead—a goal, a commitment, or an optimistic joy of life. Describe how much you trust the power of God to do his resurrection business.

## SCRIPTURE TO PONDER

*"I am the LORD, the God of all mankind.*
*Is anything too hard for me?" (Jeremiah 32:27)*

## SUGGESTED PRAYER

*Dear Lord, you are the God of all mankind. There is nothing too hard for you. Today I, _____, humbly thank you for the power you have poured into my life in the past, and I pray expectantly to see evidence of your power in my life today and in the future. I invite you to display your majesty through my smallness. Remember me, your humble servant, who willingly bows to you and loves bragging about all you have done for me.*

So . . . What Insight, Prayer, or Action Step
Has God Laid on Your Heart Today?

*Day* 21

# Weighing Everything, What Do You Want Out of Life?

Considering every possible aspect of your life, what do you want? This is not a trick question, but a basic one that must be answered by any person who wants to "end up somewhere." There's an old adage: "If you don't know where you're going, any road will get you there." So, before you travel any farther down any ol' road of life, ask yourself: "What is most important to me, and am I on the right track to get it?" Have fun for a moment and pretend that you could have one wish granted, but only one. What would you ask for? You may have to wrestle with your answer more than once on the pathway to purpose.

## Your Wish Is My Command

What do you want? Is it a month-long cruise to places you have only dreamed about visiting; a large home with a new car of your choice parked in the garage; adventure; passion; hope; or health? What takes top billing: a peaceful life, fulfilling career, or your child's safety? What would *do it* for you? Family harmony, your parent's salvation, a simple thank-you, or a fresh start? Would you set your sights on revenge, significance, success, a big dream, or a life that glorifies God? Cheri Fuller, author of *When Mothers Pray* and *The One Year Book of Praying Through the Bible*, has some good advice on this topic.

## CHERI FULLER FIGURED OUT WHAT'S IMPORTANT TO HER

Cheri is a prolific, award-winning author and inspirational speaker whose thirty-six books and messages (on topics including child development, fear, and prayer) renew the hearts of people in the United States and abroad. She enjoys writing for numerous magazines, encouraging readers to pursue a deeper experience with God and become all he created them to be. She's a wife and mother of three grown children.

Though busy by nature, Cheri has discovered that through quiet prayer, she can know God, not just know about him. She is grateful that prayer paves the way for God's grace and power to come into her life and the world around her. Cheri's passion is to inspire people of all ages to catch a vision for the impact worldwide prayer can have. In particular, she loves equipping moms and dads for the important mission of praying for their children as their first priority in parenting.

After weighing everything, Cheri is sure that what she wants most out of life is a relationship with God and people, rather than recognition. She wants to live a life surrendered to the Lord, following him and obeying him wherever he takes her. And, she wants to eliminate completely the drivenness she once was caught up in. She says she has discovered that when she gives herself to God as a living sacrifice (Romans 12:1), letting

Jesus live through her, speak through her, and love others through her by his Spirit, life is a great adventure!

She adds, "Nothing compares to the greatness of God. Nothing! When you come to the conclusion that God is worth everything, I guarantee you, you will want nothing more in life than to live in his presence!"

## Weighing Everything, What Do You Want Out of Life?

### The Magi Knew What They Wanted Out of Life

The wealthy and prominent magi traveled from afar to bring gifts to Jesus, the new king of Israel. Read Matthew 2:1–12. When you get to heaven, what question might you want to ask these men about their discovery of Jesus as the Savior of the world?

## SCRIPTURE TO PONDER

*Whom have I in heaven but you? And earth has nothing I desire besides you. My flesh and my heart may fail, but God is the strength of my heart and my portion forever. (Psalm 73:25–26)*

## SUGGESTED PRAYER

*Dear Lord God, whom have I, _____, in heaven but you? Transform my heart, Lord, so that earth has nothing I desire more than you. My flesh and my heart may fail, but you are the strength of my heart and my portion forever. Today I pray that I will live a life of loving relationships, surrender, and obedience to you. Thank you for hearing my request as I humbly petition you for what I would like most out of life.*

**So . . . What Insight, Prayer, or Action Step Has God Laid on Your Heart Today?**

# What Strength of Yours Can Easily Become a Weakness?

Have you ever thought about the fact that, before you even realize it, one of your strengths could become a weakness? Is that a frightening thought? How does that happen? You've heard stories of how someone with a superior intellect figured out how to beat the system or how someone of notoriety became deceitful. How can you guard against any type of craziness like this happening to you? It is only by becoming aware of your strengths and asking for God's protection of those strengths to be used for his glory and his plan for your life.

## Look on the Flip Side

Think about this: good looks or wealth can lead to pride. Excessive privilege can invite hardheartedness and injustice. Leadership can turn into control or manipulation. Generosity can lead to overspending on others. Physical strength can turn into abuse. Friendliness can turn into inappropriate flirtation. Obsessive planning can destroy spontaneity and cause rigidity. Ruth Graham has a great personal example of a strength becoming a weakness.

## RUTH GRAHAM CAN BE TOO KIND

Ruth is the youngest daughter of Ruth and Billy Graham and calls herself the Graham that has traveled a different path. In her recent book, *In Every Pew Sits a Broken Heart*, she shares graciously and honestly about her struggle through divorce; parenting her children through their own difficulties, including teenage pregnancies, drug abuse, and an eating disorder; the darkness of depression; and the challenge of reinventing herself at age forty. Ruth is transparent and honest as she brings a new and biblical perspective to her journey of faith, presenting a real God for real life.

Ruth is real in her faith. No easy answers. No platitudes. Currently the Lord is teaching her more about trust. And he is giving her many opportunities to do just that! For Ruth, the crux of faith is to "trust in the dark," when she is outside of her comfort zone. For her, faith is a "hold on tight" kind of lifestyle—like Jacob at Peniel as he wrestled with the Lord.

She feels she is called to be a channel of God's grace, to minister his mercy, restoration, and healing to those who are hurting, often alone and in silence. Her desire is to create a safe place for others, encouraging them to let down their masks so that healing and restoration can take place.

Ruth has one strength that easily becomes a weakness. She is caring and compassionate, but the flip side of this strength is her failure to set healthy boundaries. When people take advantage of that, she ends up feeling used and unsure of how to correct the situation lovingly. Once she hired a worker for a project. When the worker's child was tragically killed, Ruth felt deep compassion, and rightly so. But over time, in her compassion, she did not set limits and expectations so it was not long before she felt taken advantage of. Rather than confronting the person directly, she simply refused the worker's services again. In retrospect, she sees that she and the worker both lost out in the long run.

She says, "We take pride in our strengths. Very often they are God-given gifts and he desires to see us operate in them. But there is the danger that we will become self-sufficient or abuse these strengths, using them in ways he does not intend. Our strengths become our comfort zones and we refuse to let God stretch us beyond those areas that make us feel secure. Sometimes he forces us out of these comfort zones away from our strengths so that we learn in new ways to depend on him."

## What Strength of Yours Can Easily Become a Weakness?

## Some Roman Soldiers Had a Strength That Became a Serious Weakness

The Roman soldiers who arrested Christ and nailed him to the cross were strong men who were given much authority. Yet they chose to abuse their power, letting it turn into extreme cruelty. Read Matthew 27:27–31. As you reflect on their story, imagine yourself as one of the soldiers. What do you notice?

## SCRIPTURE TO PONDER

*Woe to those who go down to Egypt for help, who rely on horses, who trust in the multitude of their chariots and in the great strength of their horsemen, but do not look to the Holy One of Israel, or seek help from the LORD. (Isaiah 31:1)*

## SUGGESTED PRAYER

*Dear Lord God, woe to me, _____, and to those who go anywhere else for help, who rely on anyone else, who trust in numbers or great strength of anything else, but do not look to you, the Holy One of Israel, or seek help from you. Today I pray that I will be intently aware of my responsibility to use my strengths wisely and to devote them wholly to your glory.*

## So . . . What Insight, Prayer, or Action Step Has God Laid on Your Heart Today?

_____

_____

_____

_____

_____

_____

_____

_____

# What's Going On in Your Quiet Time with the Lord?

You are probably familiar with most of the traditional methods of having a successful quiet time. But the *what you do* is not the only important part of today's question. That would make this exercise too easy. The tougher and more important question is this: *How* have you been doing lately in your times with the Lord? God is extremely interested in the heart you bring into the experience. Do you invite the Lord into your quiet time and allow him to determine what each encounter becomes? If so, these will be some of the most treasured times of your life— when God reveals more of himself and his plans to you.

## Private Meetings with Jesus

There are many ways to enhance your quiet time: writing in a journal; confessing sin; memorizing Scripture; singing; working through a devotional guide like this one; practicing silence; enjoying God's "outdoor artwork"; or praying with praise, confession, gratitude, or requests. Are you dragging yourself into Jesus' presence and enduring a legalistic obligation? Or are you ecstatic to have the privilege of visiting with him to praise him, learn more about him, and see what assignments he has for you? Is your heart cold or on fire for your Savior? Jean Driscoll, a Paralympian, took a long time to get all of this straight in her own mind, but she knows it was well worth the effort.

## Jean Driscoll Needed Advice

Jean may have been born with spina bifida (the failure of a baby's spine to close properly during pregnancy), and she may use a wheelchair, but she is a recognized and celebrated world-class athlete. She is the only person in the 100+ year history of the Boston Marathon to ever have won the event eight times. She won silver medals in the marathon in the 1992 and 1996 Paralympic games and was named #25 of the "Top 100 Female Athletes of the 20th Century" by *Sports Illustrated for Women* magazine. Jean retired from her professional career in 2000.

The Lord softened Jean's heart toward him in 1992 through the guidance of an athletic administrator at the University of Illinois. Since that time, Jean has been active in her church and also has teamed up with the Fellowship of Christian Athletes, as well as Joni and Friends, a Christian organization that helps those with disabilities. Jean is currently a speaker and author. She has been featured on Christian television programs such as Robert Schuller's *Hour of Power*, Pat Robertson's *700 Club*, and Canada's *100 Huntley Street*.

Jean may have grown up amidst the frustration and confusion of having spina bifida, but she now recognizes physical, mental, spiritual, and emotional strengths that developed because of her body's weakness. She is grateful that her success in athletics has given her a far-reaching platform that she can use to encourage and empower people struggling with so many of life's tough issues.

Jean doesn't try to hide the fact that she used to feel that her quiet time had to be structured and done the same way all the time. She worried that if she didn't do it the way she was first taught, she wouldn't get as much out of it as she should. She was liberated, however, when she began talking with other people about their times with the Lord, and she learned that these precious moments with God can be enriched through many different methods.

She says, "God longs for us to seek him out. He wants us to speak to him and spend time with him listening. Visit with him often!"

## What's Going On in Your Quiet Time with the Lord?

_____

_____

_____

## Anna Had a Really Long and Meaningful Quiet Time!

For years, the widow Anna never left the temple. Read Luke 2:36–38. She spent her days and nights worshiping, fasting, and praying. Try to imagine that for a moment. In what way does it help you stretch your thinking about what's realistic along these lines for your life?

_____

_____

_____

## SCRIPTURE TO PONDER

*[Jesus said,] "Here's what I want you to do: Find a quiet,
secluded place so you won't be tempted to role-play before God.
Just be there as simply and honestly as you can manage. The focus
will shift from you to God, and you will begin to sense his grace."
(Matthew 6:6, MSG)*

## SUGGESTED PRAYER

*Dear Lord God, I know what you want me, _____, to do:
Find a quiet, secluded place where no one but you is watching me,
so I won't be tempted to "put on airs," pretending to be someone
I'm not when I am with you. You want me to just be there as
simply and honestly as I can manage. I know that the focus will
shift from me to you and that I will begin to sense your grace.
I pray that the time I spend with you today is the most incredible
time possible. Make me always mindful of the privilege of being
with you. And help me realize that I need to "refuel" more often,
because I'm "running on empty" too much of the time.*

**So . . . What Insight, Prayer, or Action Step
Has God Laid on Your Heart Today?**

*Day* 24

# What Do You Need to Confess?

Is there anything easy about confessing a sin? No. But skipping today's question won't move you any closer to fulfilling God's plan for your life. It would, in fact, be a terrible idea to say, "O God, you've just got to help me with my purpose in life," all the while refusing to turn away from sin. Today is a good day to confess your sin(s), which simply means to "agree with God." Let him receive your confession today, before you lay any requests at his feet.

## Not a Pretty Picture

What is your most unrelenting sin? Is it hatred, cheating, stealing, hoarding, or a judgmental attitude? Is it lying, gossip, infidelity, or impatience? Are you struggling with an obsession or a sense of entitlement? Are you harboring bitterness in your heart? And who would want to go before the throne of God to admit her laziness, addiction to drugs or pornography, or martyr syndrome? See how Michelle McKinney Hammond, cohost of the Emmy-nominated talk show, *Aspiring Women*, has dealt with her sinful nature.

## MICHELLE MCKINNEY HAMMOND AGREES WITH GOD

For years, Michelle couldn't figure out how she could have such a successful advertising career, yet continually flounder in the area of love relationships. This led her on a journey in search of perfect love, but what she found was not quite what she expected: she fell in love with God as her spouse! Today, she has become a nationally known author, speaker, singer, and television cohost, as well as the president of HeartWing Ministries.

Michelle teaches women, both single and married, how to develop more intimate and fulfilling relationships with God and others. Michelle wishes that every woman could discover the joy that comes from having a romance with the Lover of her soul. She strives to communicate the Word of God in a practical manner, so that others can experience victory in their lives in the area of singleness and everyday relationships.

Years ago, Michelle confessed her anger and her doubt that God could heal her broken heart. God heard her confession and restored her trust in him. Today, she confesses that her sin of being a people-pleaser causes her to overcommit herself, which leads to feelings of resentment when she has been stretched too thin, which leads to more guilt about not having the right attitude. She thinks she may be getting better, though, about not overcommitting in the first place.

She says, "Confession is the only path to deliverance and restoration. It reveals the painful reality of how undone we really are and what changes need to be made in our lives. It's actually quite liberating to see our situation through God's eyes, because he always includes hope in the picture."

## What Do You Need to Confess?

---

### Ezra Confessed

Ezra, a prophet and a man of integrity, cried out to God on behalf of the Israelite men who had disobeyed God by marrying foreign wives. Ezra 9:6 captures his prayer: "O my God, I am too ashamed and disgraced to lift up my face to you, my God, because our sins are higher than our heads and our guilt has reached to the heavens." Read Ezra 9:6 again and then 10:1–17. On whose behalf, yours or someone else's, do you cry out to the Lord most often?

---

## SCRIPTURE TO PONDER

*When I kept silent, my bones wasted away through my groaning all day long. For day and night your hand was heavy upon me; my strength was sapped as in the heat of summer. Then I acknowledged my sin to you and did not cover up my iniquity. I said, "I will confess my transgressions to the LORD"—and you forgave the guilt of my sin. (Psalm 32:3–5)*

## SUGGESTED PRAYER

*Dear Lord God, when I, _____, kept silent, my bones
wasted away through my groaning all day long. For day and
night your hand was heavy upon me; my strength was sapped
as in the heat of summer. Then I acknowledged my sin to you
and did not cover up my iniquity. I said, "I will confess my
transgressions to the Lord"—and you forgave the guilt of my
sin. I pray that I will renew my relationship with you today
through faithful confession of those things that are blocking me
from fully experiencing your love. You know how much I love
you and how sorry I am for my sins. Forgive me as I readily
agree with you about my sins.*

## So . . . What Insight, Prayer, or Action Step Has God Laid on Your Heart Today?

*Day* 25

# WHERE HAVE YOU SEARCHED FOR SIGNIFICANCE?

God created you to feel significant in his eyes, but most women don't focus on the "in his eyes" part of that sentence. They search for significance through their writing, speaking, teaching, or philanthropic gestures. What about you? How have you attempted to leave your mark of significance? Today is all about being significant in God's eyes—the only place his gift of fulfillment can be redeemed. Settling this issue will free you up to serve Christ more wholeheartedly.

## THE INCESSANT CALL OF SIGNIFICANCE

Over the centuries, good people have tried every conceivable method to have their life labeled as significant. They have sought stardom, completed risky goals, left architectural legacies, created memorable artwork, amassed wealth, destroyed enemies, and broken achievement records. They have been passionate environmentalists, creative lobbyists, dedicated humanitarians, superstar athletes, brilliant scholars, and stunning actresses. Some have found the secret of true significance in Jesus, but many have not. Tracy Hanson, a member of the

Ladies Professional Golf Association (LPGA) can save you some legwork on your search.

## Tracy Hanson Searched and Found What She Was Looking For

Tracy has played competitive golf for more than twenty years. Since joining the LPGA tour in 1995, she has had numerous top-five and top-ten finishes, including a tie for first place (she lost in a playoff ). Tracy ranks in the top one hundred on the LPGA all-time career money list.

Early in Tracy's spiritual journey, she knew God intellectually. However, in 1997, a broken engagement and the death of her mother took Tracy to her knees before God with a broken heart. As God nestled her close to him during this difficult time, Tracy began a heart relationship with him, and this has made all the difference in her life. Being a professional golfer provides her a unique platform to share her testimony about God's love and her personal relationship with Jesus Christ.

Tracy acknowledges that, for years, she tried to find significance through her academic and athletic achievements, but she found only discontentment amidst the success and materialism. She now realizes that her true significance is not based on how well she performs on the golf course or in any other area of her life, but on being a daughter of the King. She says, "The only significance that will not fade away is being a child of God through the grace of Jesus Christ on the cross."

**Where Have You Searched for Significance?**

## Solomon Searched for Significance

Solomon, the richest and wisest man in the Bible (with wisdom second only to Jesus), searched and searched for the truth about living a life filled with significance. Read Ecclesiastes 12:9–14. In what way do you agree or disagree with Solomon's findings?

_____

_____

_____

### SCRIPTURE TO PONDER

*This is what the LORD says: "Stand at the crossroads and look; ask for the ancient paths, ask where the good way is, and walk in it, and you will find rest for your souls." (Jeremiah 6:16)*

### SUGGESTED PRAYER

*Dear Lord, this is what you say to me: "_____, stand at the crossroads and look; ask for the ancient paths, ask where the good way is, and walk in it, and you will find rest for your soul." I humbly ask you to bless my efforts to put you first in my life today. Guide me in my understanding of you as being the only one who is truly significant and the only one who will make my life matter. Teach me to lay my worldly attempts at your feet and seek you first.*

## So . . . What Insight, Prayer, or Action Step Has God Laid on Your Heart Today?

# What Would You Like to Change About Yourself?

Have you watched any of the television programs that feature extreme makeovers of people or homes? It's interesting to see surgeons nip and tuck; beauty and fashion experts update hair, makeup, and clothing; interior designers de-clutter and remodel; and individuals and families rejoice in the changes. But what truly important thing about yourself (*not* related to your body or home) would you like God to help you change? Ask yourself: "How does God want to transform me? What change in my life would please him?" Is there something God has laid on your heart to change that will actually prepare you well for your life mission? What newness do you think is right around the corner for you?

## Change Happens

Any changes on your horizon? Are you thinking about asking God to help you walk away from a life-threatening compulsion or circumstance? Are you attempting to see your body as God's temple? Do you need courage to go to a professional counselor? Do you need more confidence to ask someone to pray for you or to support you financially while you're on a mission trip? Are you ready to live a simple, downsized life; stop abusing credit cards; walk away from an unhealthy friendship; or add more laughter and play into your schedule? Are you sensing that God is asking you to quit rehearsing your past hurts? Would he like you to polish up your writing or editing skills? Do you think he wants you to be more loyal to your friends; to become more involved in your teenager's life; to mind your own business; or simply to start obeying more traffic laws? Cheryl McGuinness, founder of Beauty Beyond the Ashes Ministry, asked God to change her tear-filled eyes into focused eyes that can clearly see his vision for her life.

## CHERYL MCGUINNESS WANTS TO CHANGE THE THINGS SHE CAN

As a result of the September 11, 2001 terrorism attack on America, Cheryl is now a widow and a single mom of two teenagers. Her husband Tom was copilot of the first airplane forced to fly into the World Trade Center. Cheryl says, "My life is not my own. I will be what God wants me to be, and I will go where he leads me." Cheryl says that she established her ministry in memory of her husband and all who died on 9/11. Today, she is a speaker and author who encourages others.

Cheryl is not shy about mentioning a change she would welcome in her life. She says that she wants to see more clearly—through her Father's eyes. She wants to see the truth about the good and the bad that happens in daily life, so she can help others understand it. She is attempting to make this change by getting to know God better and love him more deeply. She says, "God is turning the ashes of September 11th into something beautiful as I trust him with my feelings. Change is so hard, but as I surrender more, he strengthens me more. I offered up to my Lord what I considered the best part of me—my soul mate, my husband Tom—and I rise out of the ashes as God builds me anew. If I can grow through change, you can."

## What Would You Like to Change about Yourself?

### Rahab Desired Change

Rahab, the pagan harlot (innkeeper), and her family were spared by the Israelites, because she chose to change her thinking, her heart, and her actions. She decided to acknowledge and trust God by agreeing to hide Joshua's spies. Rahab's changed behavior literally saved her life and the life of her family members. Read Joshua 2:1–24; 6:17–25. In what way has change been difficult for you?

---

### SCRIPTURE TO PONDER

*Do not conform any longer to the pattern of this world,*
*but be transformed by the renewing of your mind. Then you*
*will be able to test and approve what God's will is—his good,*
*pleasing and perfect will. (Romans 12:2)*

## Suggested Prayer

*Dear Lord, help me, _____, not to conform any longer to the pattern of this world, but to be transformed by the renewing of my mind. Then I will be able to test and approve your good, pleasing, and perfect will for my life. I don't want to live in denial anymore about what needs to change. I do want you to open my eyes, but I don't know how to be brave about all this. Today I pray for the courage and strength to change the things about me that will please you. I trust you to do the transforming work in me, in spite of any excuses or resistance on my part.*

**So . . . What Insight, Prayer, or Action Step Has God Laid on Your Heart Today?**

*Day* 27

# WHEN HAVE YOU TAKEN
# A QUANTUM LEAP OF FAITH?

Quantum leaps of faith are those financial, emotional, physical, or spiritual risks that take an enormous amount of courage (without abandoning the common sense the good Lord gave you). Each risk signals a decision you make to trust and obey God with your future, no matter how difficult his marching orders. God offers intense adventure and high rewards as you open your heart to the fullness of what he has in mind for you!

## GIGANTIC LEAPS

Have you dared to take the first step toward a dream that is tugging on your heart or to ask for what you want in spite of your fear? Have you given generously in complete faith to your church's building fund, or perhaps, forgiven the unforgivable? Have you risked being judged by others when you pursued an impossible goal, adopted an HIV-infected toddler, or changed careers in midlife? Have you dared to exchange numbness and boredom for a pulse? Have you shared your testimony about God's power in your life? Have you leaped across cultural or generational barriers to solve a neighborhood problem, or jumped into a brand-new church ministry? Did you think outside the box for a solution or do something you never had considered doing before? Liz Curtis Higgs, author of a bestselling Bible study, *Bad Girls of the Bible*, and bestselling novel, *Thorn in My Heart*, took a quantum leap and is a sweet testimony to God's faithfulness.

## Liz Curtis Higgs Took a Huge Risk

Liz, a former "bad girl," is the author of twenty-two novels, nonfiction books, and children's books with nearly three million copies in print. Liz believes deeply in Jesus who lavishes us with grace. She invites people to "Come meet a man who forgives sins. Even mine. Even yours, Beloved." She loves to combine storytelling and Bible study with the goal of connecting women's and children's hearts with the grace-filled love of Christ.

Liz took a quantum leap of faith in 1995 when she realized that it was time to press beyond writing humor and encouragement pieces, which come easily to her, and begin to write biblically based fiction, which does not. Fiction requires much more of her: more book research, more heart research, and more time, money, and tears. She says, "Leapin' on your own is not only scary, but dangerous. But a true leap of faith means letting go of what's safe, secure, and predictable—and landing in the arms of our Lord Jesus, trusting him to catch you. Believe me, if he is the one calling you to take the jump, he's already got his arms open wide!"

## When Have You Taken a Quantum Leap of Faith?

### Esther Took a Quantum Leap

Esther asked that all the Jews of Susa join her and her maids in a three-day fast, before she approached the king to beg him not to annihilate her people. She said, "And if I perish, I perish." Read Esther 4:1–5:3. What risk is God asking of you in this season of your life? On a risk scale of 1 = *It's not too bad*, 3 = *This is tough*, or 5 = *I may perish*, where would you rank it?

### SCRIPTURE TO PONDER

*By faith Abraham, when called to go to a place he would
later receive as his inheritance, obeyed and went, even though
he did not know where he was going. (Hebrews 11:8)*

### SUGGESTED PRAYER

*Dear Lord, just like you called Abraham to go by faith, call me,
_____, to a place I will later receive as my inheritance.
I want it said about me that I obeyed and went, even though I
did not know where I was going. Today I pray that I will rely on
your Word as I face decisions. I ask specifically that you will give
me the needed wisdom to know exactly what to do and when to*

*do it. I ask that you would ignite a spirit of faith-based
risk in me as your bold and devoted disciple. Nudge me more
powerfully than you ever have before! I promise to stop looking
down at my safety net as I traverse across the next high wire.
You are my safety net, and I trust that you will be there to catch
me if I fall.*

**So . . . What Insight, Prayer, or Action Step
Has God Laid on Your Heart Today?**

# Where Is Your Current Mission Field?

Many believe that the term "mission field" only refers to being on foreign soil in a persecuted country. But the truth of the matter is that your mission field is where God is directing you to serve today, where he is assigning you a current role. If today's question is difficult for you, you may not be seeing the obvious answer right in front of you. Or, it may be that you would prefer to skip some of your current, ordinary tasks and tackle something magnificent for God. Are you concerned that your present role isn't worthy enough to be classified as a life mission, but just something you got stuck doing? Or, do you love your present mission so much that you are afraid you won't be willing to move on when God wants to use you elsewhere?

## Mission Fields

Where are you doing the Lord's work? To answer that question, focus on the faces across the dinner table from you or across the hallway at the office. Or, think about situations like these: Are you babysitting a few children for a single mom in your neighborhood? Do you love visiting the sick in the hospital? Did you recently go on a medical mission trip to eastern Europe? Where has God asked you to show up lately? Is it at the local, national, or global level? Are you involved in a good work, cross-culturally or interdenominationally? Do you have a ministry with an age-specific group? Lindy Boone Michaelis, the second daughter of Pat Boone, had carved out a great life for herself, when her new mission field suddenly seemed to drop from the sky.

## LINDY BOONE MICHAELIS SERVES ON THE FRONT LINES OF HER MISSION FIELD

Lindy, a wife, mother, and singer was challenged by the tragedy of her oldest son, Ryan, who at age twenty-four fell three stories through a skylight. With her father and others, Lindy has been interviewed on the "Larry King Live" television program many times since the accident to discuss the power of prayer and faith in a crisis situation. Lindy's miracle is that her son, who desperately wanted his life to point others to Christ and salvation, did not die or remain comatose. Ryan is on a slow but miraculous road to recovery, being raised up by the Lord, who has displayed his healing on the international stage.

Largely because of Ryan's sweet commitment to the Lord both before and after his accident, Lindy says she began to hunger for her own commitment to be renewed. One day, as the family was having a Bible study around Ryan's bedside, she marveled at what a mighty work the Lord had done in her life and in the lives of many others through her son, who was then silent and expressionless.

Lindy's current mission field now requires that God minister to her constantly through his Word and presence, as she cherishes, with the loving heart of a mother, this opportunity to be Jesus' hands and feet in caring for her son on an around-the-clock basis. Ryan's accident has created a platform for Lindy to point to the power and glory of God. She shares with others that what Jesus wants most is to reconcile us to himself and to help us believe that he is who he says he is.

She says, "Whatever mission field you are called to serve on, at home or abroad, remember that when we are missionaries for Christ and living in Jesus, focused on the assignment he has given us, we can have peace no matter what happens."

### Where Is Your Current Mission Field?

### Paul and Silas Worked Faithfully Wherever God Assigned Them

At midnight, after an earthquake that could have freed Paul and Silas from jail, they shared the gospel with their jailer. Before daylight, the jailer and his family were baptized. Read Acts 16:25–40. Are you as accepting as Paul and Silas of your own current mission field, or are you grumbling about it?

## SCRIPTURE TO PONDER

*[Jesus said,] "In the same way that you gave me a mission in the world, I give them a mission in the world." (John 17:18, MSG)*

## SUGGESTED PRAYER

*Dear Lord Jesus, in the same way that God gave you a mission in the world, I ask you to reveal to me, _____, a mission in the world, whether at home or abroad. Today I pray that I will learn to serve more faithfully on my current mission field. Guide me joyfully into the assignments you planned for me before the beginning of time. Minister to me, as I minister to others in your Holy Name.*

## So . . . What Insight, Prayer, or Action Step Has God Laid on Your Heart Today?

# Other Than God and Your Family, What Do You Value Most?

It is easy in a busy society to lose sight of what's really important. That's why it's critical to stop periodically and take stock of what you hold dearest. Ask yourself today what you value most, other than what many consider the most obvious—God and family. Your checkbook register, credit card receipts, and daily calendar will give you significant clues. A great, secondary question to ask yourself is this: "Will I let God use what I value to accomplish his purposes?"

## Most Valuable Award

What gets top billing in your book: a six-figure salary, designer clothes, antique furniture, an expensive "toy," or leading-edge technology? Do you most value opportunities to serve others or to tell others about Jesus' love? Do you place the highest worth on liberty, excellence, time, truth, or your spiritual transformation process? Your friendships probably rank high on your values list, but do you place great value on your small group or your church leaders? Kay Rader, former world president of women's organizations for The Salvation Army, has had her values engraved on her heart for many years.

## Kay Rader Has Sorted Through Her Valuables

Kay and her husband, Paul, raised their three children as they served God in Korea for twenty-two years. After thirty-five years of service together, both stateside and abroad, Paul became the fifteenth General of The Salvation Army, and Kay served alongside him as president of women's organizations. In 1999, she became the "first lady" of Asbury College in Kentucky, where her husband is president. She is an adjunct faculty member for the E. Stanley Jones School of World Mission and Evangelism at Asbury Theological Seminary. She also is a freelance speaker.

As a five-year-old, Kay confessed her sins and asked Jesus into her heart during family devotions with her parents. She says, though, that the ensuing years ran the gamut from high-highs to low-lows, from victory to simple discouragement to crushing defeat. At age thirty-nine, she had a spectacular spiritual encounter during which she claimed Galatians 2:20 as her own: "I have been crucified with Christ and I no longer live, but Christ lives in me." It changed her life, giving her an assurance of salvation and a hope for getting through the tough days that has not wavered since.

That experience of full surrender and Holy Spirit empowerment prepared her for an ever-enlarging ministry of teaching, preaching, and leadership. She has been intentional in her desire to serve women, particularly to help them realize their full potential for ministry.

Other than God, her husband, their family of three children, three "children-in-love," and seven grandchildren, Kay says that relationships, health, freedom, nature, the lives of unborn babies, and intellectual pursuit are all high on her list of what she values. One of her favorite passages is Matthew 6:19–21, which says that the most valuable things we can desire are treasures laid up in heaven. Kay says, "All good things on earth are to be enjoyed, but holding them loosely works best— for where your treasure is, there your heart will be also."

## Other Than God and Your Family, What Do You Value Most?

## Lydia Made Her Value a Priority

Lydia was a successful businesswoman and the apostle Paul's first convert in Europe. She so valued her faith that she hosted the new church that was formed in the city of Philippi. Read Acts 16:11–15. After you are deceased, what do you suppose non-family members will think you valued above all else?

## Scripture to Ponder

*[Jesus said,] "What good would it do to get everything you want and lose you, the real you? What could you ever trade your soul for?" (Mark 8:36–37, MSG)*

## Suggested Prayer

*Dear Lord Jesus, your words are clear that I, _____, am to value you and your truth. You say, "What good would it do to get everything you want and lose you, the real you? What could you ever trade your soul for?" Today I ask specifically that you will help me prioritize my values, so I can store up treasures in heaven. I thank you in advance for your faithfulness in doing that for me.*

### So . . . What Insight, Prayer, or Action Step Has God Laid on Your Heart Today?

# What Equipping Do You Still Need for God's Work?

God has everything you need to complete the assignments he gives you. On a moment's notice, he can send you whatever you require. So, what is it you need to do his work on earth? Talk to him about it today. God is waiting for you to ask for his help. Ask him to give you the tools, abilities, people, and supplies you need. Rely on his infinite possibilities when you start to get overwhelmed with your finite amount of time, insight, or grace toward others. That which is impossible for you is possible with God. Ask him to prepare you well for your life mission.

## You Need What!?

What do you need most? Is it discernment about who to trust, or is it vision, courage, or financial resources? God can provide you with a loving support system, energy, and even a platform. Do you need permission from some key person to proceed? Do you need a spiritual mentor to help you comprehend your sufficiency in Christ? Do you need more faith, clarity, knowledge, or balance in life? Do you want to ask God for more creativity, compassion, or for a strategic plan or a ministerial network? Ask him for what you need today. Is it the development of your character (for example, confidence or reliability) or the development of spiritual habits (tithing, fasting, or a simple lifestyle)? Barb Lindquist, the world's top-ranked female, professional, Olympic distance-triathlete, figured out exactly what she needs and now she is asking for it.

## BARB LINDQUIST NEEDS SOMETHING MORE

Barb was a world-ranked swimmer at Stanford University during her college years. She feels blessed that triathlons exist, because she loves to swim, bike, and run. Triathlons, like all sports, are performance-based, and Barb admits that it's a very human reaction to get feelings of self-worth from racing well. But God has shown Barb that he loves her no matter how she races. Living this truth takes away the pressure of racing well and frees her to express the athletic abilities God has given her. Triathloning is Barb's mission field! She travels around the world, training and racing for God's glory—and telling fellow triathletes and sports fans how much she loves Jesus.

Barb says that she still needs God's boldness to do his work better. She knows that in unfamiliar social settings, she can be shy and quiet about God's extravagant love for her, instead of radiating his boldness. She adds, "God gives each of us unique abilities. Then he equips us with extra blessings (like boldness, time, money, etc.) to maximize our work for him. We please God when we ask to be equipped and when we rely on his strength—not our own."

# What Equipping Do You Still Need for God's Work?

### David Needed Equipping

When David went out to meet the giant Goliath, he chose not to wear a helmet and coat of armor, but he went equipped with the power of the Lord Almighty. Read 1 Samuel 17:32–51. When you fight "giants," what do you always like to take with you?

## SCRIPTURE TO PONDER

*And now, may the God of peace, who brought again
from the dead our Lord Jesus, equip you with all you need
for doing his will. (Hebrews 13:20-21, NLT)*

## SUGGESTED PRAYER

*Dear Lord, I pray now that you, the God of peace, who brought
again from the dead our Lord Jesus, will equip me, _____,
with all I need for doing your will. In fact, today I ask
expectantly for a dramatic equipping to do your work on earth
and serve you more completely!*

## So ... What Insight, Prayer, or Action Step Has God Laid on Your Heart Today?

# WHAT'S MISSING IN YOUR LIFE?

On Day 30, we focused on what equipping you still might need to do God's work. Today, let's take a slightly different approach and hone in on yet-to-be-satisfied personal wants or wishes. Ask yourself: "What would make my life more complete?" Has the lack of it upset you for years? Have you cried your heart out over it? God cares about what you have to say today and about how you feel. Don't let any sadness or frustration in this area steal opportunities from you to live the glorious life God has planned for you.

## MISSING IN ACTION

Have you ever felt like filing a "missing in action" report about one of these: hope, friendship, love, dreams, passion, clarity, integrity, or goals? Is one of these missing: spiritual growth, a date night with your husband, play days with your children, downtime for yourself, an organizational system? Is family unity, a Sabbath rest, personal joy, or a college fund for your children missing? Is it health, income, or a much-anticipated marriage proposal? Let Lori Salierno, CEO of Celebrate Life International (CLI), speak wisdom into your life today through her story.

## Lori Salierno Gave God Her Heartache

Lori is the founder of CLI, a nonprofit organization that promotes leadership skills and character development among students in public schools and the juvenile justice system. She is a nationally-known speaker who has written four books, including *Real Solutions for Ordering Your Private Life*.

Lori says that her spiritual life is "an adventure and a party combined." Her goal is to glorify God and enjoy him forever. She is in the process of introducing her God-given teen leadership program, Teach One to Lead One, into fifty-one thousand high schools across the United States, as a means of cultivating the hearts of seventy-two million teenagers for a relationship with Jesus Christ.

What's missing for Lori? She says, "My husband and I have been married for twenty-two years and have not been able to have children. But God actually took away my desire to be a birth mother and replaced it with an incredible passion for at-risk students. He did this by placing an intense call on my life to reach our nation's children in this generation. What an awesome privilege to be used in this way." Lori summarizes: "God can use the things that are missing from our lives (even the absence of children) to bring glory to his name. I'm a good example of his faithfulness in tough situations!"

## What's Missing in Your Life?

_____

_____

_____

### Eve Felt Something Was Missing

Eve wanted to be more like God, and so she succumbed to temptation in the Garden of Eden. Read Genesis 3:1–6. Like Eve, have you searched after something that you thought was missing in your life, only to discover that you wished you hadn't found it?

_____

_____

### Scripture to Ponder

*"For I know the plans I have for you," declares the LORD,*
*"plans to prosper you and not to harm you, plans to give you*
*hope and a future." (Jeremiah 29:11)*

## SUGGESTED PRAYER

*Dear Lord, you know the plans you have for me, _____.*
*You have declared that they are plans to prosper me and not to*
*harm me, plans to give me hope and a future. Today I thank*
*you for your well-thought-out plans for my future. I also pray*
*about what I perceive to be missing from my life. Help me today*
*to give my missing piece(s) to you with confidence that you will*
*use my apparent lack for your good and holy purposes. I know*
*you see the bigger picture, and I trust you to fill my void with*
*your presence. I choose to live a life of gratitude about what I*
*do have, rather than a life of sadness about what I don't have.*

## So . . . What Insight, Prayer, or Action Step Has God Laid on Your Heart Today?

# What Do You Want to Be Doing for God Ten Years from Now?

Imagine what your life would look like in the next five to ten years if you dedicated yourself to becoming the woman God designed you to be and to accomplishing something enormous *for* him and *with* him. Today, let's focus on the second half of that question: accomplishing something. Do you daydream about what he wants of you? What if you flipped that idea upside down and allowed yourself to reflect on what *you* want to do for *him*? That's not considered selfish thinking, by the way, because God is the one who instills wholesome musings in our hearts. What gift could you give to God that would make your heart sing? An even better way to phrase that question is this: What gift will God give to you and through you to the people he is sending you to serve? Whatever it is, remember that, if God has purposed it, it will happen.

## What Long-Term Plan Has God Laid on Your Heart?

Do you find yourself talking to anyone who will listen about the day you can establish a mentoring program for pregnant teens, campaign against indecent television shows, begin a local ministry for families who have an incarcerated parent, start a church in an impoverished rural area, or teach your grandchildren about Jesus? Are you anxious to start an intercessory prayer team at your church or, more boldly, to help put prayer in public schools? Do you have plans to become a licensed marriage, family, and child counselor or a foster parent for chemically dependent babies? Lisa Winters Cox, one of television's original Doublemint twins, loves the daydream God gave her years ago.

## Lisa Winters Cox Is Looking Forward

Lisa has moved from a career of television spots and modeling to a ministry that includes speaking, teaching, writing, and dramatic arts. She is a wife, mother, actress, and dancer. She says, "Although I am a genetic copy of my identical twin, I have discovered that I was created for a unique spiritual purpose."

Lisa explains that she recently had to let go of her fear and pride and stop saying, "You've got the wrong woman, God!" Now she says, "Here am I, Lord. Send me." She is on the creative arts team at her church, and she is writing and teaching her first Bible study, *That I Might See: A Look at the Healing Miracles of Jesus.*

What would Lisa like to be doing for God ten years from now? She hopes to be ministering with her immediate family and mother, as well as her two sisters and their families. They know that they are called by God to encourage those who need spiritual and emotional healing. They have an incredible blend of gifts, talents, and training; and they envision a retreat/conference/arts center. Lisa comments: "God did not put long-term daydreams in our hearts to frustrate us. They are there to pull us ever closer to him and to his great plans for our lives."

## What Do You Want to Be Doing for God Ten Years from Now?

### Solomon Made Long-Term Plans with God

King Solomon and his laborers spent seven years building the temple of the Lord in Jerusalem. (This does not account for the many years King David spent in preparation to build.) Read 1 Kings 6:37–38. Even if the project had taken Solomon and his crew fifty years, do you think they should have undertaken it? Why?

### SCRIPTURE TO PONDER

*We constantly pray for you, that our God may count you worthy of his calling, and that by his power he may fulfill every good purpose of yours and every act prompted by your faith. We pray this so that the name of our Lord Jesus may be glorified in you, and you in him, according to the grace of our God and the Lord Jesus Christ.*
*(2 Thessalonians 1:11–12)*

## SUGGESTED PRAYER

*Dear Lord Jesus Christ, I constantly pray that God may count me, _____, worthy of his calling, and that by his power he may fulfill every good purpose of mine and every act prompted by my faith. I pray this so that your name, Lord Jesus, may be glorified in me and me in you, according to your grace. I also pray today that my heart and mind will be filled to overflowing with "impossible" plans that you have already chosen for me to fulfill. Look with favor on me, as you guide me into the miracles you designed for me. Let me stand amazed at your plan and strategy for my life.*

**So . . . What Insight, Prayer, or Action Step Has God Laid on Your Heart Today?**

# WHAT WEAKNESS OF YOURS HAS GOD TURNED INTO A STRENGTH?

A weakness is a good thing when you give it to God to use for his glory, and he turns it into a strength! Has that ever happened to you? If so, did you bow and give credit to Almighty God? It's a treat of a lifetime to watch God in action. There are few experiences like it in this world. Trust him to turn your weakness into a strength, so you can better fulfill your mission.

## A WEAKNESS = A GOOD THING?

Has God transformed your insecurity and fear of public speaking into an unexplainable, roaring courage, which reflects your trust and confidence in who he is? Has he been so creative as to take your loud personality and give you a love of auctioneering? Has he used your extreme shyness as a perfect complement for the role of a gentle, quiet hospice chaplain? Was your doubt in yourself changed to faith in him? Has he funneled your hate into championing justice for the oppressed? Did he reveal to you how large your ego had become, causing you to be humbled? Did he show you the ugliness of your impatience, causing you to crave patience? Babbie Mason, Dove award-winning songwriter and singer, needed God's intervention to breathe his strength into her weakness.

## BABBIE MASON HAS SEEN GOD AT WORK

Babbie is a recording and concert artist, with fourteen albums and a host of Dove awards to her credit. She is a wife, mother of two adult sons, and doting grandmother of one darling baby girl. Babbie is grateful to have closely observed the lives of her parents, who were deeply committed to Christ. She says that they made it easy for her to fall in love with him and call him Lord. She tried to imitate them in their love for God and service to others, and she worked alongside them in the church that her father pastored.

For as long as Babbie can remember, she knew that her assignment from God would involve music. But she says that she was well into adulthood before she really began to understand that the music he instructed her to write and sing transcends race, culture, and denominations. She is now certain that God is using her music to bring worshipers together as his family. She says, "What a beautiful sight it always is to see the body of Christ in worship. It's dress rehearsal for heaven!" She believes her job is to rally the troops. She feels that the members of the body of Christ have been wounded and beaten down by life in general. She reminds them that, although life takes us from one test to another, we have Christ, the best Teacher available, to help us pass each one.

How did God turn a weakness of Babbie's into a strength? She once had a horrible fear of flying until God used a very dear friend to remind her that although the enemy tries to target and torment us, God has power to protect us and accomplish his plans. It was a real time of spiritual growth for Babbie, and her "return to the air" gave her a bold personal testimony to share about the magnificence of God. She says, "God's grace is sufficient for every weakness. When you come face to face with weakness, it is not the time to back down and surrender to feelings and emotions. That lack of trust is like saying to God, 'I don't think you'll come through for me, so I'll take matters into my own hands.' Instead, bathe yourself in the Word of God. Memorize it. Go with what you know about the eternal God, not with how you feel at the moment. And ask him to give you his strength."

## What Weakness of Yours Has God Turned into a Strength?

## The Disciples at Pentecost Had a Weakness That Was Turned into Strength

On the Day of Pentecost, 120 disciples—scared, ordinary men and women—were gathered in an upper room in Jerusalem, waiting for Jesus (who had ascended into heaven) to send "power from on high." He did so in the form of the Holy Spirit, who filled the disciples with a boldness they had never known before. Read Acts 2:1–13. With what weakness do you need Jesus to help you? Do you want him to make you a bold evangelist like the disciples or do you have a different request in mind?

## SCRIPTURE TO PONDER

*But he said to me, "My grace is sufficient for you,
for my power is made perfect in weakness." Therefore I will
boast all the more gladly about my weaknesses, so that
Christ's power may rest on me. (2 Corinthians 12:9)*

## SUGGESTED PRAYER

*Dear Lord, you said to me, "My grace is sufficient for you,
_____, for my power is made perfect in weakness."
Therefore, I will boast all the more gladly about my weaknesses,
so that your power may rest on me. I am so grateful that you
know my shortfalls and that you are willing to take me from
where I am today, powerfully using the not-so-good parts
of me for your plan. I pray that I will learn to release more
of my weaknesses to you. Help me, when I feel inadequate,
to remember that I can trust you to be strong.*

**So . . . What Insight, Prayer, or Action Step
Has God Laid on Your Heart Today?**

# How Balanced Is Your Life?

One of the greatest oxymorons of the twenty-first century is a balanced life. It's as silly as saying jumbo shrimp. There are simply too many domains of life: personal (finances, leisure, relationships, and education), family, faith, church ministry, vocation, and community to keep all the balls in the air at one time. So, let's make sure that today's question is realistic: Think about whether the top three domains of your life are somewhat balanced with a reasonable amount of downtime in between. Simply ask yourself: "Is my life balanced enough to hear God's plan for my life and carry out what he'd like me to do?" Some days will be better than others, but each day is a brand-new day. Try to make balance more of a habit than an exception. Aim for a simple lifestyle and a content heart.

## Are You Part of the Great Balancing Act?

We can't be all things to all people, but many of us try to be! Do your obligations include being part of the "sandwich generation" (caring for young kids at home as well as aging parents)? Do your commitments resemble any of these: being a girls' softball coach, preparing for a board meeting, taking a class, or serving as a lay minister at your church? Do you attend parent-teacher nights, go to the movies with a friend, host bridal and baby showers in your home, or try to communicate regularly with your husband? Are you keeping the Sabbath holy each week? Sandy Bloomfield-Demelli, a former finance business executive, struggled with this issue of balance as much as anyone, as she sought God's will for her life.

## SANDY BLOOMFIELD-DEMELLI COULDN'T DO IT ALL

Sandy joyfully ministers to both Jews and Gentiles through praying, as well as through writing and speaking about the healing, resurrecting power of Jesus. She has cofounded a Bible study for people in the show business industry, produced Christian events and documentaries, and interviewed top Christian leaders for magazine features. She also hosts a weekly television program, *Rocking the Foundations*, which is broadcast in the Philadelphia area as well as the Caribbean.

Sandy is the daughter of a Jewish father and Protestant mother, and she loves teaching on the Hebrew roots of her Christian faith. She feels that this provides both cultural context for much of Jesus' teachings and scriptural keys for what remains ahead for believers. She says that she gives the Lord full access to her time, relationships, possessions, vocation, and daily decisions.

For years, Sandy's life was not balanced; her career and ministry overshadowed all other domains of her life. Then, she grieved the loss of her mother to cancer and soon afterward got married after forty-two years of being single. It was then that she began learning firsthand the meaning of balance, as she underwent a complete reordering of her priorities. She melded agendas with her new husband in a new city with new friends in a new season of life. Sandy quickly discovered a great peace by acknowledging that we need both the north wind (blustery, cold busyness) and the south wind (gentle, warm times alone) to release the fullness of our life's fragrance.

She says, "To hear from God about how to live a balanced life daily, we need to spend time on *holy ground*, continually praying and seeking his will. We must do that before we take our place on the *battleground*, dealing with the demands and unexpected challenges of life. Just as manna was given to the ancient Israelites on a daily basis, it is only through day-by-day prayer that the Father shares his thoughts about balancing our life domains."

## How Balanced Is Your Life?

## The Proverbs 31 Woman Lived a Balanced Life

The woman described in Proverbs 31 is wise, moral, and God-fearing. She is a virtuous wife and mother, resourceful entrepreneur, and friend to the poor. (And then there are the rest of us!) Read Proverbs 31:10–31. Have you ever had a good cry over not being able to keep up with this ideal woman? How about simply focusing on living a balanced life as best as you know how today?

## Scripture to Ponder

*And Jesus matured, growing up in both body and spirit,*
*blessed by both God and people. (Luke 2:52, MSG)*

## Suggested Prayer

*Dear Lord Jesus, help me, _____, to follow your example*
*of maturing and growing up in both body and spirit, blessed*
*by both God and people. I pray that you will breathe wisdom*
*into me to help me with this tightrope balancing act of life.*
*You know how much I struggle in this area. I know that the*
*time I spend listening to you is fundamental to creating and*
*maintaining balance.*

## So . . . What Insight, Prayer, or Action Step Has God Laid on Your Heart Today?

# What Do You Need to Learn?

God likes to use those who are teachable. He looks for people who are lifelong learners. He needs women who are willing to learn new techniques, styles, processes, and skills, as may be necessary to do his work. What is it that would help you complete all the purposes God has planned for you?

## Lifelong Learner

What's the most important thing you need to learn? Is it parenting skills, Scripture memorization techniques, or moderation? Is it communication skills, so you can be a better spouse; time management skills, so you can be a better steward of God's time; or boundary and margin training, so you can say no to other people's goals for your life? Do you need some help in overcoming a fear, learning how to relax, or being intimate? Do you need a deeper knowledge of God, Jesus, the Holy Spirit, the Bible, or church doctrine? Do you need to learn how to relate better to people, when to speak up, or how to speak a foreign language? Do you think it would be helpful if you knew more about human nature or picked up some leadership pointers? Would you feel better prepared if you learned more about the specific field in which you hope to make a contribution? Thelma Wells, an author and keynote speaker for the Women of Faith conferences, loves learning new things.

## THELMA WELLS TEACHES OTHERS WHAT GOD HAS TAUGHT HER

Thelma is a Christian mother to people all over the world. Her goal is to inspire, encourage, influence, and empower others to be their best for Christ. She estimates that she speaks to more than 400,000 women each year. As an inspirational speaker, Thelma delivers this formula for success: B + E + E = S. (**B**e aware of who you are + **E**liminate the negatives in your life + Work for **E**ternal Value. That will = **S**uccess.) She has the privilege of sometimes traveling with her adult daughters as a ministry team.

Thelma has been a Christian since she was four years old. She believes in the promises of God and in the entire Bible as his unerring Word. She asks daily to be clothed in his righteousness.

Thelma says that although she just completed a degree in theology she needs to learn more about the sovereignty (supreme power and authority) of God through his Son, Jesus. And she says, "One of the most critical things to learn in this life is to trust God with everything—the good, the bad, and the ugly."

**What Do You Need to Learn?**

**Thomas Needed to Learn Something**

Doubting Thomas needed to learn to trust Jesus. Read John 20:24–28. How are you doing in the trust department?

## SCRIPTURE TO PONDER

*"I will instruct you (says the Lord) and guide you along the best pathway for your life; I will advise you and watch your progress."*
*(Psalm 32:8, TLB)*

## SUGGESTED PRAYER

*Dear Lord, instruct me, _____, and guide me along the best pathway for my life. Advise me and watch my progress. Today I want to acknowledge that you are the only true source of all wisdom and knowledge, and I so appreciate your patience with me as I learn about you, your love, and the life you want me to live. Make me more teachable day-by-day. I want to learn how to better represent you. Help me set realistic goals about what I should focus on learning next.*

## So ... What Insight, Prayer, or Action Step Has God Laid on Your Heart Today?

# WHAT IS YOUR UNHEALTHY METHOD OF ESCAPE?

Most women have at least one unhealthy method of escape that numbs the pain of tough realities. What about you? Oh, you say that your escape technique is under control and inactive right now! Well, in that case, please note that even a dormant volcano has the potential to erupt and spew lava. In fact, the minute you claim to have overcome an escapist tendency, it will probably pop up again more dramatically or recruit a worse temptation to substitute for itself. Be willing to see the truth today. Facing this head-on can change your life forever. Ask yourself: "What happens to my self-control when I feel the need to escape? What is camouflaging itself as a treat when, in reality, it's a trick to keep me from God's best?"

## ESCAPE METHODS ACTUALLY TRAP YOU

Where do you go when you want to escape? Track your footsteps. Follow your trail for a minute. Do you go to the refrigerator to eat junk food, the mall to spend money you don't have, the telephone for long gripe sessions, or the liquor store for booze? Do you seek perfectionism in assignments to feel in control or watch television programs day and night to hide from reality? For some women, inhaling nicotine takes them to a numbing place; for others, it's smoking marijuana or popping pills. Do you rage at your children, view internet pornography, watch a violent movie, read a trashy romance novel, or have an affair—all to gain momentary relief from pressure? What's the dangerous game you play with your destiny? Karen Hill, a children's author, is a bit of an expert on this topic. Listen to what she has learned.

## KAREN HILL LET GO AND LET GOD HAVE HIS WAY

Karen is a bestselling children's author as well as assistant and editor for another bestselling author—Max Lucado. Karen was raised by parents who were devoted Christians and was strengthened by their Rock of Gibraltar-type of faith. Her heart has always belonged to her Savior, and for him she would do anything. Currently she knows that his plan for her life is to help young people accept the unconditional love of God and to help Max accomplish his unique assignment.

Karen's most destructive method of escape is workaholism. Her high need to accomplish her goals and be productive keeps her running back to her desk day and night. The good news is that God has now blessed her with three loving grandchildren, and they are ever-so-diligently teaching her how to relax in the most delightful ways—simply by being together. They are instructing her in the lost art of playing.

She says, "When we women feel compelled to keep everything running smoothly and to solve everyone's problems, we overlook our own emotional, spiritual, and physical health. It's then that we are tempted into unhealthy methods of escape. Sometimes rest or play is the holiest of choices. A balance of *being* and *doing* is the key, and that's what I'm trying to learn. Even Jesus, as busy as he was, took time to be alone in prayer with his Father and attend a wedding celebration!"

**What Is Your Unhealthy Method of Escape?**

_____

_____

_____

### The Pharisees Had an Unhealthy Method of Escaping from Truth

The Pharisees escaped into a world of legalism, which allowed them to ignore the need for loving relationships. Jesus criticized their crutch of hiding behind the law. Read Matthew 23:1–33. It's not pretty! What do you think are the two most common ways women avoid the truth about themselves or their circumstances?

_____

_____

_____

### SCRIPTURE TO PONDER

*Teach me to see what I still don't see. Whatever evil I've done,*
*I'll do it no more. (Job 34:32, MSG)*

## SUGGESTED PRAYER

*So, dear Lord God, teach me, _____, to see what I still
don't see. Whatever evil I've done, help me to do it no more.
Today I ask you to help me admit my unhealthy escapism and
avoidance tactics and to stop hiding in them. I am tired of the
severe consequences they cause in my life. Guide me into your
freedom, especially when I try to dull the pain in an illegal or
immoral way or to run away into oblivion. Teach me how you
want me to rest and play, always remembering that you are
the only true restoration of my spirit.*

## So . . . What Insight, Prayer, or Action Step Has God Laid on Your Heart Today?

# WHEN HAVE
# YOU OBEYED GOD?

Radical obedience to God means you obey him immediately and joyfully, doing whatever he tells you to do. It means you are so surrendered to his will that you are able to go wherever he leads, whenever he says. It is most often a learned behavior that develops over time, after many years of daily practice of responding to his easy requests. In what ways has God asked you to obey him today? Have you done what he asked of you? Are you beginning to understand that learning to be more and more reasonably obedient right now is simply practice for the radical obedience he will require of you to complete your life purposes?

## ARE YOU REASONABLY OR RADICALLY OBEDIENT?

When have you practiced obedience? Did you help your grouchy neighbor, tithe faithfully to your church, go to seminary, or invite an unbeliever to an Easter service? Did you do so immediately and joyfully? Did you start a ministry that was heavy on your heart, become more of a servant-leader to your coworkers, or confess and repent of a sin? Has God asked you to be more patient in line at the bank, get up an hour early to pray, give up your golden idol of status, or prayerfully fast from soda for a month? Have you felt led to encourage your pastor, refrain from negative comments, or house a church intern? Kathy Collard Miller, author of *Princess to Princess*, had learned over a ten-year period to obey God in many ways, except one major area.

## KATHY COLLARD MILLER HATED HER DISOBEDIENCE

Kathy is a popular women's conference speaker and best-selling author of forty-seven books on topics including perfectionism, simple lifestyle, and what's in the Bible for couples and teens. She has spoken in twenty-eight states and five foreign countries. She is married to her now—best friend, Larry, and has two grown children. And, she loves to reach out to people through friendship evangelism.

Kathy longs to share hope with others, because, as she humbly discloses, "God delivered me from being a child abuser." Even though she had been a Christian for ten years at the time, she couldn't grasp God's strength to control herself. She felt unloved, unable to comprehend why her husband was not home more often to help raise their two young children and give her the emotional support she craved. Feeling overwhelmed, she displaced her anger from Larry onto their two-year-old daughter and soon considered suicide as the only solution for the harm she was inflicting.

Kathy's step of obedience at that point was not easy. God asked her to share publicly about her sin of physically abusing her child. She didn't want to at first, of course, but when she did step out in obedience, she saw God's amazing plan unfold for her ministry of healing. She says: "God only desires our good and his glory, so even if he asks us to obey in something that seems difficult to us, his great power can bring good from it."

## When Have You Obeyed God?

## Mary Obeyed

When Mary found out that she was to be the mother of Jesus, she said, "I am the Lord's servant. . . . May it be to me as you have said." Read Luke 1:26–38. How do you typically react to obeying God's will for your life? Like Mary?

### SCRIPTURE TO PONDER

*[Jesus said,] "If you love me, you will obey what I command."*
*(John 14:15)*

### SUGGESTED PRAYER

*Dear Lord Jesus, you said, "If you, _____, love me, you will obey what I command." Today I ask you to help me be courageous in following you wherever you lead, whenever you say, and for whatever assignment you give me. Don't let me*

*delay in my joyful response to your will. I want to do this because
I love you, but I do admit that I am grateful for the freedom,
peace, and mind-boggling rewards that come from obeying you!
Help me listen to you more closely and obey you more radically.*

## So . . . What Insight, Prayer, or Action Step Has God Laid on Your Heart Today?

# WHEN HAVE YOU EXPERIENCED GOD'S TIMING IN YOUR LIFE?

God's timing is always perfect, and he has known your every need and action since before you were born. But that's not easy to believe when you're in the middle of a situation that you feel strongly shouldn't have happened or should turn around immediately. Have you ever felt that God must be asleep, that he's just not doing his job? Focus today on the fact that God is never a nanosecond early or late. Think about a situation in which he was enormously kind to you in his timely decision to act on your behalf. And, by the way, always remember that thanking God in advance for his best timing speaks loudly of your trust in him. He will reward you for listening for his timing in the unfolding of his plan for your life, rather than impatiently running ahead of him.

## GOD'S PERFECT TIMING

Did you witness God's great timing in regard to a court ruling or a business contract? Did you feel his wisdom when you became aware of your spouse's illness, were offered a chance to study abroad, or found illegal drugs in your teenager's room?

Or, have you chuckled after-the-fact about God's timing when he did not grant what you asked for when you wanted it? He knows when you need to meet a new friend or come to a realization. He knows when you need to be ready to champion a cause or practice restraint. He knows, better than you, when the timing is right for a birth, death, or the discovery of a new medical procedure. Pam Rosewell Moore, who was a personal assistant and companion for seven years to Holocaust survivor Corrie ten Boom, certainly trusted God's timing in her personal life.

## PAM ROSEWELL MOORE WAITED FOR YEARS FOR GOD'S GREEN LIGHT

Pam has led a very interesting life. From 1966 to 1967, she was secretary to the archbishop of East Africa. From 1968 to 1976, she was an assistant to Brother Andrew (author of the bestseller, *God's Smuggler*). From 1976 to 1983, she was an assistant and companion to the elderly Corrie ten Boom, a gifted speaker who had hid people from the Nazis during the Holocaust and later survived a concentration camp; and from 1988 to 2003, she was director of prayer ministry at Dallas Baptist University. She is now a speaker and writer.

Pam says she wants to listen to the Holy Spirit more closely because he knows the will of God! She sees herself as an encourager of fellow Christians, teaching them to live in abandonment to God, even if his will requires doing things that seem impossible.

Pam experienced God's timing in a powerful way. In March 1965, at age twenty-one, she pledged to God that she would never marry anyone without his consent and blessing, even though she longed for a husband and children. Twenty-one years later, to the month, she and a man who had become a dear friend, Carey Moore, both realized that they had God's blessing to become husband and wife. She says, "As we get to know God better, we begin to understand by faith that there is infallible and safe timing in every step we take in obedience to him. We simply place our weak hand into God's strong hand and trust him, even though in many cases, only he sees the perfection of his timing."

## When Have You Experienced God's Timing in Your Life?

### Sarah Witnessed God's Timing in a Powerful Way

Sarah, who had been barren all her life, was to become a mother at the age of ninety. God said that he would bless her so that she would be the mother of nations. Read Genesis 17:15–22. When have you witnessed God's timing in someone else's life?

## SCRIPTURE TO PONDER

*There is a time for everything, and a season
for every activity under heaven. (Ecclesiastes 3:1)*

## SUGGESTED PRAYER

*Dear Lord, you have reminded me today that there is a time for everything and a season for every activity under heaven. I thank you that I, _____, can trust you as my all-knowing and all-powerful God. You are the only one who could watch out for me so wonderfully, never being one nanosecond early or late in your timing. I ask you to run my life on your timeline.*

**So . . . What Insight, Prayer, or Action Step Has God Laid on Your Heart Today?**

# How Does God Get Through to You?

Does God have an easy or hard time getting your attention? What is his best method of reaching you? Did you know that God longs for you to hear him, that he's not trying to keep his will a secret? He's able to use whatever method of communication fits your personality on any given day. What if you harnessed all the energy you have spent saying, "I don't know what God wants me to do," into one incredible, extended experience of sitting quietly before the Lord and asking him to reveal his thoughts to you?

## Will You Take God's Call?

How does God reach you? Is it through his Word, by affirmation to you from a mature Christian, or with vivid impressions? Is it through your times of silence with the car radio turned off, in a small group women's study, while you are praying and fasting, or as you are journaling? Do you hear him during volunteer assignments or when you witness a crisis of someone worse off than yourself? Do you hear him during your pain or through a spiritual mentor you highly respect? Has it taken a near-death experience for you to hear him? Do you need to stop the endless chatter in your mind to hear God today? Kali Schnieders, former Miss Missouri-World (who once lost a beauty pageant competition to TV's *Wonder Woman*, Lynda Carter!), has uncovered some helpful hints about hearing God.

## KALI SCHNIEDERS KNOWS TO BE QUIET

Kali retired from a sixteen-year career in the corporate world to raise her stepdaughter, but a series of personal losses prompted her to use those experiences to encourage others. Now Kali loves to help people smile in the midst of their trials, taste God's grace, and find his best in their worst situations. Her book, *Truffles From Heaven: Discovering the Sweet Gift of Grace*, catapulted her from a beauty contestant into a popular conference and retreat speaker. She has also written *You're Not My Mom! Confessions of a Formerly "Wicked" Stepmother*.

How does God get through to Kali? She says that she is grateful that he speaks to her all day long in a variety of ways: through Scripture that applies to her situation, through nature that prompts her to stop and thank him as Creator, through other people who encourage her exactly when she needs it, and through the miracle of answered prayers. Kali sees evidence of God in the ordinary things that many people write off as coincidence. To her, every encounter (whether pleasant or not) can be used by God to draw us to him for love and comfort.

She shares, "I've discovered that God is continually speaking, but many people either don't really expect to hear him or they allow the cares of life to distract them from listening. God said, '*Be still* and know that I am God.' Unless we are willing to be still, we'll miss what he has to tell us. Sometimes I have to remind myself, 'Don't just *do* something—sit there!'"

**How Does God Get Through to You?**

_____

_____

_____

### Noah Listened to and Heard from God

Noah listened closely to God and was instructed how to prepare for a flood by building a massive ark. Noah obediently spent 120 years building that ark, even though it's likely he had never before seen rain! Read Genesis 6:1–22. Imagine these words said of you: _____ listens to God, obeys him, and finds favor in his eyes. How would that make you feel?

_____

_____

_____

## SCRIPTURE TO PONDER

*God means what he says. What he says goes. His powerful*
*Word is sharp as a surgeon's scalpel, cutting through everything,*
*whether doubt or defense, laying us open to listen and obey.*
*(Hebrews 4:12, MSG)*

## Suggested Prayer

*Dear Lord God, I, _____, understand that you mean what
you say and that what you say goes. Your powerful Word is sharp
as a surgeon's scalpel, cutting through everything, whether
doubt or defense, laying me open to listen and obey. Today I
admit that I long to hear from you on a daily basis—in fact,
on a minute-by-minute basis—in each of my decisions, projects,
and relationships. I invite you to talk to me. I want to hear
from you. I promise to practice being quiet and to listen ever
so carefully.*

### So . . . What Insight, Prayer, or Action Step Has God Laid on Your Heart Today?

# WHAT IS THE ROOT CAUSE OF YOUR ANGER?

Have you ever gotten angry with someone and then said to yourself: "What was that all about? What's really going on with me?" Have you tried to investigate what's most often the cause of your anger? Identifying and cleaning up what's beneath the surface can be a freeing experience. Answering today's question will help you begin to rid yourself of any underlying, diseased area of your life, so you can better navigate through your next God-given purpose.

## FACING A ROOT CAUSE IS AKIN TO FACING A ROOT CANAL

What ugliness is at the root of your anger? Is it pride, frustration, physical pain, or lack of control in a situation? Is it self-righteous indignation, selfishness, disgust, sadness over an injustice, or fear of rejection? Anger can be a defense against vulnerability, intimacy, or commitment; it can be a way to keep people off the scent of the truth about you. Have you figured out that your anger is often caused by exhaustion, insecurity, or disappointment? Or, could it be caused by your impatience,

186

envy, or embarrassment? Elisa Morgan, president of MOPS Int'l (Mothers of Preschoolers), has learned the value of looking beneath the surface of her anger.

## Elisa Morgan Knows There's More to the Story Than Meets the Eye

Elisa, the wife of Evan for nearly a quarter of a century and the mother of two almost-grown children, is a woman committed to growing through all that God brings her way. Since 1989, Elisa has been president and CEO of MOPS Int'l, a lifestyle-evangelism organization that nurtures moms of preschool-age children around the globe. She is also an author, speaker, and host of *MomSense* radio.

Elisa says, "God is so much better and more complex than I ever imagined. He is generally unfathomable! I love growing into the challenge of trusting him and yielding my life to him." Elisa comments that she is called to truth—to know it for herself and to share it with others. During this season of her life, her audience has been mothers. She admits that her platform has been her own inadequacy in mothering, and she is honored that God has allowed her deficits to be offered up for his purposes.

Elisa's bouts with anger are much less frequent now, but when she does get angry, she immediately digs past the surface to find out what else is really going on. She tries to determine if her anger is stemming from pain, fear, or perhaps sadness—which are probable causes for her. She has some excellent advice to share: "Anger is labeled a bad emotion, and women are told that they are not supposed to get angry. The truth is that anger is a real human emotion. Anger can be a friend when we learn what it wants to teach us, especially what has triggered it."

**What Is the Root Cause of Your Anger?**

_____

_____

_____

**Cain Had Underlying Causes for His Anger**

Cain killed his brother, Abel, in the first recorded murder in Scripture. The root cause of his anger is clearly stated in the Bible: Cain was jealous of God's favor with Abel. Read Genesis 4:1–15. How do you feel when you are on the receiving end of someone's unbridled anger?

_____

_____

_____

### SCRIPTURE TO PONDER

*My dear brothers, take note of this: Everyone should be quick to listen, slow to speak and slow to become angry, for man's anger does not bring about the righteous life that God desires. (James 1:19–20)*

## SUGGESTED PRAYER

*Dear Lord, I know that I, _____, should be quick to listen,
slow to speak, and slow to become angry. Let's face it, my anger
does not bring about the righteous life that you desire. Today
I pray that you will help me better understand what is causing
my anger, what I can learn from it, and what to do about it
as it is happening. Help my anger move me toward constructive
action, so that it will bless others, not harm them. I ask you to
give me a desire to share the truth about the root cause of my
anger with someone I trust. Save me from myself!*

**So . . . What Insight, Prayer, or Action Step
Has God Laid on Your Heart Today?**

# How Would You Spend Your Last Week on Earth?

You've probably wrestled before with the question of how you would spend your last week on earth. Was your answer that you would eat, drink, and be merry; or did you have a more serious response? If you did have one week left, would you have any regrets about whether you had discovered and fulfilled God's purposes for your life? Would you start racing around trying to get your entire life assignment accomplished in one week? There will be no need for a final flurry, if you start living today with a sense of urgency for doing God's work.

## Last-Minute Details

If you were in great health, what would you scurry around doing the last seven days of your life? Would you go to your favorite vacation spot, give away all your money and possessions, pray around the clock for unbelievers, or videotape your testimony? Would you say "I love you" or "Jesus loves you" to as many people as possible? Would you get your finances in order, make amends, sleep, or write your memoirs? Arvella Schuller, television producer of Crystal Cathedral's *Hour of*

*Power* and wife of Robert for more than one-half century, knows firsthand about living with a sense of urgency.

## ARVELLA SCHULLER LIVES AS IF THERE WERE NO TOMORROW

Arvella is in full-time, team ministry with her husband. Her responsibilities at church include programming two morning worship services and serving as video/print editor. More importantly, she is a mother of five, grandmother of eighteen, and friend of a wonderful congregation, especially its women.

Arvella grew up in a devout Christian home, and at age sixteen, she made a commitment to serve Jesus Christ full-time. She has learned to lean on her Lord through the many challenges life has brought. She considers herself privileged to share a special relationship with Jesus Christ through her music and worship, and she has no doubt that God called her to use her gifts in those areas. She also feels led to share her faith with others.

What would Arvella do with one week left to live? When diagnosed with breast cancer at age fifty, she faced a similar question: "What would I do if I only had six to twelve months left to live?" Then at age sixty-eight, after a heart attack and open-heart surgery, she bled internally. While being rushed back into surgery, she was sure she was dying, yet she was so overpowered with Jesus' presence and beauty that she did not think about her precious husband or family. That's why she says that, if she only had one week left to live, she would tell others what a joy it is to serve Jesus and to spend time alone with him. She also would thank each one of her family members for making her so proud of them for becoming the people God wants them to be.

Arvella says, "I value each new morning. I am always amazed that God has given me yet another day to live and give away his love to my husband, family, church, television ministry, and yes, of course, to the clerks in our neighborhood store, dry cleaners, and post office."

## How Would You Spend Your Last Week on Earth?

### Hezekiah Only Had a Short Time to Live

When godly King Hezekiah became deathly ill, God granted his request of fifteen more years. During that time Hezekiah trusted God even more and saw the defeat of the Assyrian army. Read Isaiah 38:1–8. What would you do with your time if you knew you had exactly fifteen years left to live?

---

### SCRIPTURE TO PONDER

*God has given us eternal life, and this life is in his Son. He who has the Son has life; he who does not have the Son of God does not have life. (1 John 5:11-12)*

## SUGGESTED PRAYER

*Dear God, you have given me, _____, eternal life, and this life is in your Son. You have made it clear that he who has your Son has life and he who does not have your Son does not have life. Today I ask you to give me a godly perspective about the temporal and eternal. Set my feet in motion as if it were my last week to affect lives for you. Help me to be grateful for every day you give me, knowing that each one is a priceless gift.*

### So . . . What Insight, Prayer, or Action Step Has God Laid on Your Heart Today?

_____

_____

_____

_____

_____

_____

_____

# What Do You Need to Surrender?

Surrendering to God is an act of humble submission. It is admitting that Jesus is Lord; that he is God and you are not. It is trusting God with every aspect of your life, to the point of submitting all to him. When you think you couldn't love God any more than you already do, try surrendering something important to him. It will be an interesting and difficult exercise, to say the least! When you can release something that you have held on to tightly, you will fall more in love with the one whom you can never outgive.

## White Flag of Surrender

God wants you to give him your despair, worry, feelings of inadequacy, anxiety, secret sin, and checkered past. He wants you to turn over to his care your aspirations, favorite pet, most expensive jewels, worst enemies, parent's failing health, and fear of being burglarized. He is to be the Lord of your job, home, bank accounts, vehicles, and even your hobbies. He is there to help you with every part of your life—your emotions, education, possessions, talents, health, awards, and more—as you surrender all to him. Would you be willing to give him your credit cards, sugar addiction, children's future, control issues, evening wine, or agenda for the day? Mary Ann O'Roark, former executive editor of *Guideposts* magazine, finally surrendered something that was simple, yet made a profound difference in how she viewed life.

## MARY ANN O'ROARK SEES A NEW FREEDOM

Mary Ann grew up on the Ohio River in West Virginia. She has memories of being nine years old, starting her own neighborhood newspaper, and dreaming of going to New York City. Since then, she's been an editor and writer for a number of national magazines, as well as a flight attendant. Now as a freelance writer and speaker, she enjoys her dream-come-true life in a Manhattan high-rise.

Mary Ann thinks of writing as a form of prayer, and she helps others to share their own stories as sacred tools of healing and encouragement. She speaks at women's gatherings, writing conferences, and church retreats around the country, guiding participants in journaling explorations to invite the Holy Spirit's joy and abundance.

After September 11, 2001, Mary Ann surrendered her notion that life is predictable or safe. That tragedy made her appreciate how the Holy Spirit works miracles amidst chaos and change—and that her role is to live lovingly and kindly, taking each moment as it comes. She says, "Surrender is letting go of our preconceived fears and resentments, so we can move ahead. It is putting aside our own ego and choosing not to be imprisoned by external events. It is saying, 'We are part of a greater universe, a greater mystery.'"

## What Do You Need to Surrender?

### Uzziah Needed to Surrender Something Big

Uzziah, a godly king of Judah, needed to surrender his pride. Because he did not, the Lord afflicted him with leprosy, and he was excluded from the temple of the Lord. Read 2 Chronicles 26:16–23. You most likely won't be struck with leprosy because of unsurrendered pride, but you will not live the life you were meant to live until you surrender all. Is it easier for you to see things other people need to surrender or to admit what you need to surrender?

### SCRIPTURE TO PONDER

*[Jesus said,] "Any of you who does not give up everything*
*he has cannot be my disciple." (Luke 14:33)*

### SUGGESTED PRAYER

*Dear Lord, I know that if I, _____, do not give up every-*
*thing I have, I cannot be your disciple. So, today I ask you for*
*wisdom about what you would like me to surrender next and for*
*the strength to turn it over to you. I pray too for daily courage to*
*surrender more and more to you. I know that the things which*

*are most difficult for me to lay at your feet are actually the things that are better off in your care and control—not mine! I know that I am only the steward of what you have given me. Help me surrender all, so that I might truly be set free in you. I trust you.*

## So . . . What Insight, Prayer, or Action Step Has God Laid on Your Heart Today?

_____

_____

_____

_____

_____

_____

_____

*Day* 43

# HOW DO YOU TRY TO STEAL GOD'S GLORY?

To steal is to take something that is not yours. To try to steal God's glory means that you are taking credit for what he chose to accomplish through you. Run from self-idolatry. Be the type of woman God loves to use to point people to himself.

## ARE YOU THE THIEF WHO GOT CAUGHT?

What tricks do you have for trying to skim off some of the praise and honor owed to God? As you graciously accept compliments for a speech, do you forget that God gave you your talent as a speaker? Or what if someone is tearfully thanking you for making meals for her family during a tragedy? Do you forget that God gave to you in abundance so you could share? Do you exude a self-aggrandizing attitude or hear yourself saying "I" all the time, as if you were meant to be the center of attention? Do you brag, wallow in the limelight, or fail to share kudos with your support team? Do you long to get credit for your good deeds? Do you harbor an ungrateful heart, arrogantly refusing to bow and say thank you to God? Do you fail to mention to others the miracles God has performed for you? Do you like being in the know, which sets you up as a little god with secret information? The next time people are complimenting you over a profound insight, will you gratefully thank God for the wisdom he gave you? Anne Ortlund, cofounder of Renewal Ministries with her husband, admits her own weakness in this area.

## ANNE ORTLUND SEES THE PROBLEM CLEARLY

Anne and her husband, Ray, have served together in ministry for decades. Their calling is to help believers love the Lord passionately and completely, and to ask those believers to help others do the same. Anne and Ray travel extensively—speaking at conferences, mentoring pastors and Christian leaders, and discipling small groups. They are now working on their twenty-seventh book.

Anne's personal passion is to love the Lord with all her heart, soul, strength, and mind, though she admits that she has often tried to steal God's glory! She says that the temptation in her spirit is to promote herself, exalt herself, name-drop, and take credit. Her struggle is continual—as in, it happens all the time! She adds, "Because of God's gracious wisdom, we can only *reflect* his glory. Praise him for that!"

**How Do You Try to Steal God's Glory?**

200

## The Babylonians Attempted to Steal God's Glory

The Babylonians wanted to make a name for themselves, so they began building a tower that would reach to the heavens (later called the Tower of Babel). They were moved with pride and ambition, preferring their own glory to God's honor. God made it perfectly clear to the Babylonians that this sin was not acceptable. Read Genesis 11:1–9. What's your earliest memory of wanting life to be all about you or wanting to make a name for yourself?

---

### Scripture to Ponder

*"And we, who with unveiled faces all reflect the Lord's glory, are being transformed into his likeness with ever-increasing glory, which comes from the Lord, who is the Spirit."*
*(2 Corinthians 3:18)*

## Suggested Prayer

*Dear God, I, _____, can only reflect your glory as in a foggy mirror. Slowly, though, I am being transformed into your likeness with ever-increasing glory, which comes from the Lord, who is the Holy Spirit. Today I pray that I will have a clearer knowledge of you, so I will yearn to reflect your glory more and more every day. Send your Holy Spirit to transform me daily to become more like you. Teach me to humbly bow to your glory.*

## So . . . What Insight, Prayer, or Action Step Has God Laid on Your Heart Today?

# How Often and How Hard Do You Laugh?

Laughter breaks the chains of perfectionism, control, manipulation, and bitterness. It also breaks down barriers with others, especially if you learn to laugh at yourself. By the way, if you can't belly laugh yet, practice! It's a stress release and a freedom worth gold. Ask God to teach you to laugh. It will help you put your life into perspective. Smile and laugh, alone and with others, every chance you get. People who need to be reached with the gospel will be less likely to respond to you if you are rigid, inflexible, legalistic, too serious, or sour-faced!

## Smiles, Chuckles, and Belly Laughing

Think about what makes you laugh. Is it your pets, wholesome comedy routines, television bloopers, or costume parties? Is it toddlers' quizzical facial expressions or your teenaged daughter's dramatic reenactment of conversations with her friends? Do you laugh at political satire, practical jokes, comic strips, or home videos? Bless others with your laughter. LeAnn Thieman, a nurse who helped rescue three hundred babies from Vietnam, got an unexpected chuckle on that particular mission.

## LeAnn Thieman Had a Good Laugh

LeAnn begins every day by reciting Psalm 25. Her favorite part is verse 4: "Show me your ways, O LORD, teach me your paths." It's that type of daily trust in God's direction that exemplifies her life. She is an author (three books in the *Chicken Soup for the Soul* series) and speaker, who shares lessons learned from the extraordinary circumstances of the Vietnam orphan airlift in 1975.

LeAnn had volunteered to escort six babies from Vietnam to their adoptive families in the United States. Organization officials then asked her to smuggle ten thousand dollars into the country to help the cause of the orphans. Shortly thereafter, the North Vietnamese army closed Saigon to external traffic and outside communication. This placed many orphaned babies and children in serious danger. Enroute to Vietnam, LeAnn had to hide all that cash in her bra, resulting in hilarious antics in the airport bathroom! When she arrived in Saigon, she was greeted with these words: "President Ford just approved Operation BabyLift. You'll be helping us take out three hundred babies!" Shaken to her core, LeAnn prayed for courage.

Among many other things LeAnn learned, what did she learn from the incident about laughter? That "laughter is a great coping skill and one of God's most awesome gifts to us. We need to create laughter every day in our lives, because unbridled joy is one of the best ways to show our gratitude to God for his love, protection, and provisions."

## How Often and How Hard Do You Laugh?

_____

_____

### The Captives Laugh

When the Jews celebrated their release from Babylonian captivity, they laughed and sang. Read Psalm 126:1–6. Are you, too, long overdue for a good laugh?

_____

## SCRIPTURE TO PONDER

*[God speaking of bringing his people back from captivity]*
*"Thanksgivings will pour out of the windows; laughter will spill through the doors. Things will get better and better. Depression days are over. They'll thrive, they'll flourish."*
*(Jeremiah 30:19, MSG)*

## SUGGESTED PRAYER

*Dear Lord Christ, you promise that when you come to reign, thanksgivings will pour out of windows and laughter will spill through doors. You say that things will get better and better; depression days will be over, and the people will thrive and flourish. Today I, _____, pray that my life right now will be filled to overflowing with smiles and laughter (from chuckles to belly laughing)—and that my laughter will be contagious to*

*those who so desperately need to put their depression days behind
them. Help me take myself much less seriously than I do you,
Jesus.*

## So . . . What Insight, Prayer, or Action Step Has God Laid on Your Heart Today?

# WHAT IS YOUR
# PRIZED EXCUSE?

God surely has heard every excuse under the sun, but if you're a parent, teacher, ministry leader, or employer, you too have probably heard some mighty fine excuses. Have you ever felt like retorting, "Well, e-x-c-u-s-e me. Just do it!" How do you think God feels about an excuse you make for not following the advice you asked him for? To defuse the power of your favorite excuse and move past it, you must first acknowledge that it does have a hold on you. Focus today on confessing your most frequent and stubborn excuses for not doing what God or others ask of you.

## EXCUSE ME!

What's your typical excuse? *The cost is too great. It's too embarrassing. So-and-so would be better at it. People will laugh at me. I'm not that smart. I'm too busy. I'm not as spiritual as you think I am. I'm not good at that. It's not my gift. I'm needed elsewhere.* Do any of these excuses sound like you? *I don't know how. I'm too afraid. I'm too tired. It takes too long. It hurts too much. You don't pay me enough to do all that. We've never done it that way before. We don't have enough in the budget.* Kathy Peel, founder and president of Family Manager, Inc., had to learn to repent of her beloved excuse.

## Kathy Peel Excused Herself

Kathy is a popular speaker; frequent guest on television and radio programs; a contributing editor to *Family Circle* magazine; and author of seventeen books on topics including stress, healthy relationships, organizing your home, and surviving school holidays. Her unique assignment from God is to equip busy women to make their home a great place to be and to empower them in their role as mom and family manager. She says that the older she gets, the less it seems she knows—and the more she longs to know God and experience in deeper ways what it means to be his child.

At times, Kathy pulls out a clever excuse that goes like this: "I can't do *it*, because *it* requires my full attention, thus preventing me from efficiently multitasking." She says, "After all, not being able to multitask makes me feel like I'm wasting time! I would rather accomplish quickly the things that I have to do, so I have more time for the things I want to do." Kathy is slowly learning that she misses opportunities to see and hear God and experience his presence and miracles when she is hurriedly crossing things off her "daily hit list." She's trying to slow down more regularly to enjoy the journey and to give important tasks her undivided attention.

She says, "I think we women have mastered the art of excuses. Any ol' excuse will do for busy, tired ladies. I believe that the only cure for a preponderance of excuses is rest, and by that I mean, resting in the comfort and peace that our Lord offers to the weary."

## What Is Your Prized Excuse?

## Moses Had an Excuse

Moses feared that he did not speak well enough to represent God. He said: "O Lord, I have never been eloquent, neither in the past nor since you have spoken to your servant. I am slow of speech and tongue." Read Exodus 4:10–17. When, like Moses, have you tried to excuse your way out of an assignment?

### SCRIPTURE TO PONDER

*The man said, "The woman you put here with me—she gave me some fruit from the tree, and I ate it." [Literally, the oldest excuse in the Book!] (Genesis 3:12)*

### SUGGESTED PRAYER

*Dear Lord, I, _____, do not want my life to be filled with excuses like, "That person you put here with me made me do it!" Today I pray that I will learn to recognize and chuckle at any and all excuses I make. I ask that you would keep me from excusing my way through life. I don't want my excuses to steer me off the adventurous path you have mapped out for me.*

## So . . . What Insight, Prayer, or Action Step Has God Laid on Your Heart Today?

# WHAT ARE YOU MOST GRATEFUL FOR?

What fills you with a deep sense of gratitude? Is it your family, friends, faith, education, food, shelter, and clothing? Today, try to focus on something that you don't ordinarily dwell on. Living a life filled with gratitude will remind you of how fondly God has cared for you in the past and present, and that he has only good plans for your future.

## LIVING IN GRATITUDE

We take so much for granted, be it our transportation, our vacations, or our health. What miracle of life are you enormously grateful for? Is it a challenge you survived that made you stronger? Is it freedom, grace, forgiveness, your job, or your pets? Are you grateful that your infant is sleeping through the night; that your children are saved and safe; or that you ended up with a great daughter-in-law? Are you grateful for your eyesight or hindsight; for the sunshine or rain; or for the unexpected second chance you got? Are you grateful for a circumstance that helped morph you into a better person, a time when you were affirmed for your talents, or a sweet childhood memory? Charlotte Smith-Taylor, a professional basketball player in the Women's National Basketball Association (WNBA), has much to be grateful for.

## CHARLOTTE SMITH-TAYLOR EXUDES GRATITUDE

Charlotte was thrilled to sink the winning shot in the 1994 national championship game, giving the University of North Carolina its first women's collegiate basketball title. She feels that she has been handpicked by God for the WNBA—to use basketball as a platform to share her faith in Jesus Christ with fans, especially children. But nothing brings Charlotte greater pleasure than to follow Christ's example of servanthood; she loves giving of herself and her time to help others.

Charlotte is grateful for every opportunity she has to share Jesus Christ because she knows that when she shares Jesus, she gives life to others. She is also grateful for a family who loves the Lord as much as she does and for the wonderful Christian husband God recently gave her. She adds, "And, I'm grateful for my favorite gospel artist, Yolanda Adams!"

Charlotte says, "Try your best to give thanks to God in everything you do. Develop an attitude of gratitude. That will help you smile and do things as though you are doing them for him."

**What Are You Most Grateful For?**

## Bartimaeus Was Grateful

Bartimaeus, the blind man, was grateful that Jesus gave him sight. After he was healed, he followed Jesus. Read Mark 10:46–52. Think about this today: Would you still be a grateful woman, even if God never did anything else for you?

---

### SCRIPTURE TO PONDER

*One of them [one of ten lepers], when he saw he was healed, came back, praising God in a loud voice. He threw himself at Jesus' feet and thanked him—and he was a Samaritan. Jesus asked, "Were not all ten cleansed? Where are the other nine?"*
*(Luke 17:15-17)*

### SUGGESTED PRAYER

*Dear Lord Jesus, your Word says that only one of the ten lepers, a lowly Samaritan amidst nine Jews, came back when he saw that he was healed. That grateful man praised God in a loud voice, threw himself at your feet, and thanked you. Jesus, I, _____, never want you to ask of me, "Were you not cleansed too? Where are you?" Today I throw myself at your feet, filled with gratitude for how you have cleansed me and for all you have done for me. I ask you to remind me constantly of all the other things I have to be grateful for. Fill me with an abundance of gratitude. I want to say thank you with my life!*

## So . . . What Insight, Prayer, or Action Step Has God Laid on Your Heart Today?

# WHAT ARE YOUR SPIRITUAL GIFTS?

Spiritual gifts can be compared to birthday presents from the Holy Spirit, because they are given by him at the time of your spiritual birth. When you joined the family of God, you received at least one divinely ordained ability—probably more. At that time, you were empowered by the grace of the Holy Spirit to be an instrument of Christian service within the framework of the body of Christ. The more you use your spiritual gifts for the health and growth of the church body, the more in touch you will become with your purposes in life. If you have never studied this topic before, here are some action steps to consider: Read *Your Spiritual Gifts* (by Peter Wagner) or *19 Gifts of the Spirit* (by Leslie Flynn). Then, you may want to set up an appointment to chat with a pastor about your questions. Don't let your gifts stay wrapped up. God wants you to use them to finish strong in the race of life.

## SURPRISING GIFTS

When you became a believer in Jesus Christ, did you receive the gift of knowledge, healing, administration, faith, or evangelism? Did you find that you had the gift of preaching, discernment, celibacy, or voluntary poverty? Were you empowered with the gift of a missionary heart, much like the apostles in New Testament times? Your gifting may be in the area of hospitality or shepherding. You may have discovered that you have the gift of wisdom or intercessory prayer. Jan Johnson, coauthor of *Dallas Willard's Study Guide to The Divine Conspiracy*, has thoroughly enjoyed the spiritual gifts the Holy Spirit selected for her.

## JAN JOHNSON WAS GIVEN GIFTS

Jan is an author of numerous Bible studies and fourteen books about Christian living. A member of the American Society of Journalists and Authors, she has sold more than a thousand articles to publications like *Woman's Day*, *Discipleship Journal*, and *Focus on the Family*. She is a wife, mother, sister, aunt, speaker, teacher, and spiritual director. She also volunteers at a drop-in center for the homeless and at Epiphany (which sponsors three-day retreats at youth correctional facilities).

Jan is interested in having an interactive life with God. In order to connect with him, she practices spiritual disciplines such as prayer, Bible study, meditation, extended times of solitude, silence, and service. As she connects with him, she says that he is ever-so-slowly transforming her into Christlikeness.

She outlines her three purposes in life right now as these: spiritual formation (connecting with God in authentic ways); compassion and social justice (caring for the throwaways of our culture as Jesus did); and helping people, especially in the American church, focus on substance over glitz (by discovering and living out God's purposes instead of living a self-absorbed existence).

Two of Jan's spiritual gifts are teaching and encouragement. She says that teaching gets to the heart of her passion, because it emphasizes the fact that she's a lifelong student of the Word. She says, "The Greek word in Scripture for 'teacher' doesn't necessarily indicate someone who's a good communicator, but rather someone who loves to study and dig deeply into topics. The Greek word for 'encourager' indicates someone who's likely to teach or exhort in an effective way." She says, "A spiritual gift is not simply limited to something you're good at. It's something that comes to you with amazing desire; it is a gift from God to be used for building his universal church. You may develop many other skills along the way, but a spiritual gift is something to get you started on fulfilling your purposes in life."

## What Are Your Spiritual Gifts?

## Stephen Had a Spiritual Gift

Stephen had the rare and beautiful spiritual gift of martyrdom. He spoke boldly and was willing to die for Jesus. Read Acts 7:54–60. How would you like to have been given the gift of martyrdom? Perhaps you have been.

## SCRIPTURE TO PONDER

*We have different gifts, according to the grace given us.*
*If a man's gift is prophesying, let him use it in proportion to his*
*faith. If it is serving, let him serve; if it is teaching, let him teach;*
*if it is encouraging, let him encourage; if it is contributing to the*
*needs of others, let him give generously; if it is leadership, let him*
*govern diligently; if it is showing mercy, let him do it cheerfully.*
*(Romans 12:6–8)*

## SUGGESTED PRAYER

*Dear Lord, each person has different gifts, according to the*
*grace you have given us. I believe that if a woman's gift is*
*prophesying, she should use it in proportion to her faith. If it is*
*serving, she should serve; if it is teaching, she should teach; if it*
*is encouraging, she should encourage; if it is contributing to the*
*needs of others, she should give generously; if it is leadership, she*
*should govern diligently; if it is showing mercy, she should do it*
*cheerfully. Today I, _____, thank you for the unmerited*
*spiritual gifting you have bestowed on me, even for those gifts I*
*have yet to discover. I pray that I will always desire to be a good*
*steward of the generous gifts you have given me. They are from*
*you and for your use. Help me cultivate them, so that I will be*
*a more useful tool in your hands!*

## So . . . What Insight, Prayer, or Action Step Has God Laid on Your Heart Today?

# What Baggage Are You Carrying That You Don't Want?

Do you feel like putting out a *For Sale* sign to rid yourself of baggage you no longer want, whether that be sins, personality quirks, annoyances, obligations, heartaches, or ineffective relationships? Be honest about what your "trash removal" wish would be. Today is the day to let go of anything you don't want, whether it's realistic or not—or whether having it in your life is your fault or not. One word of caution: You may not want to list today a cross that Jesus has asked you to bear; for example, being criticized for your faith. Or, if you are thinking of jettisoning something that God may actually want you to keep—your marriage vows, for instance—hold on. Don't be like Jonah in the Bible story that follows! Be sure you are in agreement with God about what you write. Let him speak to you today about what he wants you to get rid of as soon as possible.

## So, You Don't Want These Things?

Would you like to exchange your illness, demanding schedule, or meddling in-laws for a more perfect life? Are you ready to walk away from being abused, or from your own sin of vanity, worry, or deceit? Have you had enough regrets, unhealthy boundaries, anxiety, or bragging? Is this the last day you will curse, smoke, go to bars, or be lukewarm about your relationship with Jesus? Are you wondering how you collected so much unnecessary baggage in your life, such as jealousy, stress, or prejudice? What would you like to shed? Is it unwanted pounds, family secrets, or a guilty conscience? Dr. Leslie Parrott, a marriage and family therapist at Seattle Pacific University (SPU), has a well-thought-out list of what she's finished with.

## Leslie Parrott Wants to Throw Away Some Undesirable Things

Leslie Parrott is codirector (with her husband) of the Center for Relationship Development at SPU, a groundbreaking program dedicated to teaching the basics of good relationships. The Parrotts are authors of numerous books, including *Saving Your Marriage Before It Starts, Becoming Soul Mates,* and *When Bad Things Happen to Good Marriages.* They have been featured on *Oprah, CBS This Morning,* CNN, and *The View,* and in and *USA Today* and the *New York Times.* They have two sons.

Leslie's call is to "transform relationships to transform lives." She works side-by-side with her husband Les to provide books and seminars that help to make bad relationships better and good relationships great. They draw from cutting-edge psychological research and sound biblical wisdom, combining them to give practical insights that enhance relationships, with a special emphasis on marriage.

Leslie says, "I was in my late twenties when my parents suddenly divorced after thirty-five years of a seemingly happy marriage. It was my dad who left to remarry and create a new family. His sudden leaving was an unhappy shock and in my grief and anger I withdrew from him. Consequently, an entire decade passed without seeing my dad. I wince to even say those words. Even though we have now reestablished our relationship, those lost, cold years between us haunt me deeply. It is the heaviest baggage I carry.

"I'm betting most moms can relate to my 'mommy baggage.' I seem to accumulate doubts and fears on a near daily basis (am I praying for the boys enough?; why did I use that tone of voice?; and so on). These are the nagging voices that weigh me down with regret like too many suitcases at the airport!

"It is the heavy baggage of our 'shoulda, coulda, wouldas' that pulls us into the past and robs us of joy and aliveness in the present. When we open the window to the fresh breeze of God's grace, his mercy really is 'new every morning.'"

### What Baggage Are You Carrying That You Don't Want?

### Jonah Had Something He Didn't Want

Jonah had a direct calling from God that he did not want. So, he fled on a ship bound for Tarshish, instead of heading to Nineveh where he was supposed to go. Read Jonah 1:1–3:3. What about you? What might you be trying to get rid of that God may want you to keep?

222

## SCRIPTURE TO PONDER

*Scrub away my guilt, soak out my sins in your laundry.*
*(Psalm 51:2, MSG)*

## SUGGESTED PRAYER

*Dear Lord, there are things in my life that I, _____, don't want. For example, God, I ask you to scrub away my guilt and soak out my sins in your laundry. And even though I say today that I don't want certain things, Lord, you and I both know that they have filled a need in my life up to this point—so, now help me to fill that hole with you. I pray that I will have more of what you want me to have in my life. Take from me thieves that rob me of my laughter and joy—and help me accept crosses that perfect me. Help me live a life that pleases you, stowing my baggage with you!*

## So . . . What Insight, Prayer, or Action Step Has God Laid on Your Heart Today?

_____

_____

_____

_____

_____

_____

# To Whom Has God Called You?

First and foremost, God has called you to himself—to get to know him, love him, and glorify him. But has he also called you (asked you to follow him and obey him in a specific way) to minister to a particular group or certain age range of people? For whom does your heart break? Whose cries echo in your ears? Few thrills compare to the discovery of your life's calling, including specifics about who, what, where, or how you are asked to humbly serve. If you have already heard the details about to whom you are called, jot that down today in thanksgiving. If not, ask the Lord to reveal to you ministry opportunities to the general population, as you prayerfully surrender to his will and await further instructions from him.

## Have You Heard the Call?

Do you gravitate toward church pastors who are computer illiterate, anxious to teach them how to prepare a PowerPoint presentation? Has God specifically urged you to pray for the lepers in Calcutta, India, or to support the orphans in Tijuana, Mexico? Do you feel compelled to visit those in jail? Do you ache for children who have special needs, for your church's youth ministry, for those adults with no church family, or for visiting missionaries? Are you a friend to unwed mothers, the homeless, elderly, oppressed, fatherless, or widows? Are you drawn to those who are indigent, fire victims, orphans, hearing impaired, house-bound, or war veterans? Do you feel led to work with a parachurch organization to reach the unsaved around the world? Renee Stearns, an attorney, wouldn't trade God's call on her life for all the money in the world.

## RENEE STEARNS RECEIVED AN EARLY CALL FROM GOD

For twenty-eight years, Renee has been the wife of her college sweetheart, Rich, who is president of World Vision US. Before starting a family, Renee served as a legal services attorney for the poor. Over the years, she has raised five children and been active in church ministry as a speaker and teacher. God has given Renee the privilege of partnering with him to accomplish his purposes in the world, whether that is to take a stand against the AIDS epidemic, feed the poor, or comfort widows and orphans.

If you had asked Renee, as a child, what she wanted to be when she grew up, she would have clearly told you, "I don't want to be a nurse or a teacher. I only want to help the really poor people." Since becoming a Christian in her teens, Renee has learned that her relationship with Jesus Christ is a lifelong process of growth and development. She knows that it is far more than a spiritual veneer; it is a journey of obedience to Christ and his Word. This attitude continues to take her deeper in her knowledge and understanding of who God is and what he desires for her life. She loves looking to him daily for her next step.

She says, "What breaks my heart is that too many people refuse to accept the call, because they feel that the world's problems are too overwhelming and that their contribution would be insignificant. The truth is that God is watching to see what we will do with what he has given us, no matter how much or how little that is."

## To Whom Has God Called You?

## Philip Was Called by God

Philip, the evangelist, was one of seven men chosen by the apostles to serve the early church by ministering to the Greek-speaking widows and the poor. He also was given another targeted assignment, this time from an angel of the Lord who said: "Go south to the road—the desert road—that goes down from Jerusalem to Gaza." Philip obeyed God, met an Ethiopian, and baptized him upon the man's request. Read Acts 6:1–6 about the widows and Acts 8:26–40 about the Ethiopian. Philip was called specifically to minister to widows and to an unbeliever. In what general way is Philip's calling also our calling as Christians?

## Scripture to Ponder

*[God said,] "Before I formed you in the womb I knew you,
before you were born I set you apart." (Jeremiah 1:5)*

## Suggested Prayer

*Dear God, before you formed me, _____, in my mother's
womb you knew me, before I was born you set me apart. Today
I pray that you will continue to direct my footsteps. Work in my
life, so that I can more clearly hear to whom I am called. Help
me as I yearn to know my next step on the journey of serving
others.*

**So . . . What Insight, Prayer, or Action Step
Has God Laid on Your Heart Today?**

# What Current Activity or Opportunity Might Be a Distraction?

Human beings like to avoid pain and find pleasure. Distractions help with that, whether they involve procrastinating about honoring a deadline or diligently focusing your energy on some worthy cause to hide from one of the heavy responsibilities that God sent you into the world to do. Today's topic really starts with this question: Have you embraced a distraction as a clever way to hide from God's next task? If you have, who can blame you? He assigns some tough jobs! Distractions can make you feel satisfied, important, safe, or too busy to respond to God. It may comfort you to know that women who face dragons and earthquakes on a regular basis in their family's lives often find themselves easily distracted by the easier, softer side of life. It's a survival instinct, a pressure release valve! Other bored women want to escape the severe reality of ordinariness and get lost in the magnificent, extraordinary business of running the universe, or at least, minding someone else's exciting business for a little while. It's a way to get their pulse back. Commit today to eliminating any distractions that are keeping you from God's best.

## What Distracts You under the Sneaky Guise of a Worthy Activity or Opportunity?

Are you easily distracted from major tasks because of emails, phone messages, Instant Messages, text messages, faxes, or junk mail? Do you find that you overemphasize dining out and other entertainment, or that you abuse television for the sake of resting your brain? Are you the self-appointed gossip for your neighborhood, family, or office? Are you obsessing over what your body looks like or spending countless hours bidding on eBay for things you don't need or can't afford? Do you find yourself championing causes that others are passionate about? Ask yourself: "What is it that I tend to take on as my own task, when someone else could or should be doing it?" Are you wasting time worrying? Here's a harder question: Are you serving in ministry to actually avoid important, pressing responsibilities at home? Kathy Ross ministers through Reasons to Believe, an organization that links cutting-edge science to the Word of God. She fights daily against succumbing to distractions.

## Kathy Ross Understands the Desirability of Distractions

An enthusiastic adventure-lover, Kathy thrives on challenges. In 1986, she applied her experience as an educator and communicator, to assist her husband, Hugh, in launching Reasons to Believe. In addition to adoring her family, friends, and pets, she continues to work alongside Hugh as an editor and executive.

Kathy loves to dig into Scripture, uncover new insights, and lead others to discover truths. From time to time, she teaches a Bible class or leads a retreat for her interdenominational, evangelical church. She says she feels led to ignite and fan the spark of people's passion for learning truth, which gives them a zest for life and zeal for leading others to faith in Christ.

Kathy confesses that she is easily distracted by the many unmet needs for leadership that she sees around her—in her job, local schools, community, church, and so on. Each time she notices something lacking, she has a strong desire to try to fulfill that need, instead of focusing on what God specifically has called her to do.

She says, "A godly man once observed that people who take too much responsibility for others' lives and projects do so to stay busy enough to blissfully ignore some of their own responsibilities. So when my life loses focus or gets off track, I look to see how I'm ignoring or neglecting something in me or near me."

## What Current Activity or Opportunity Might Be a Distraction?

## Nehemiah Knew How to Handle Distractions
Nehemiah wisely stayed on task even when his enemy, Sanballat, manufactured a supposedly urgent problem to distract him. Read Nehemiah 6. How much prayer do you think is needed to grow into that Nehemiah-type wisdom and discernment regarding distractions?

## SCRIPTURE TO PONDER

*Jesus replied, "No one who puts his hand to the plow and looks
back is fit for service in the kingdom of God." (Luke 9:62)*

## SUGGESTED PRAYER

*Dear Lord Jesus, you have said that if I, _____, put my
hand to the plow and look back, I am not fit for service in the
kingdom of God. Today I pray that I will not be like a plowman
who looks back or looks away from his task and then ends up
cutting crooked furrows. Guide me into a life-changing analysis
of my current distractions to your plans. Help me to see the
truth about all the possible scripts available for my life and to
choose only yours. I sincerely want to adjust my schedule to fulfill
roles you have assigned to me and accomplish goals you have
designed for me. I want to weed out everything else.*

### So . . . What Insight, Prayer, or Action Step Has God Laid on Your Heart Today?

# How Do You Prioritize Your Roles and Goals?

Roles in life (student, employee, neighbor, wife, mom, lay minister, and so on) are difficult to manage because of the sheer volume of responsibilities that accompany them. Then, throw into the mix the idea of goal-setting on a regular basis, as you try to sort out what God's next step is for you. It's enough to drive you crazy or at least cause severe panic attacks. The only way to stay sane is to understand *how* to prioritize all of it. So today I want you to think about your favorite method of prioritizing. Be honest with yourself, because by prayerfully thinking about that, you will be able to see the value or fallacy in your current approach. Think about how you have done life in the past, and then focus on how God intends for you to get organized around his priorities for your life.

## There's So Much to Do and So Little Time!

How do you prioritize? Do you do whatever is urgent or answer whoever screams the loudest? Do you use sticky notes to help you remember what you need to handle, or sort through bills to see which ones are almost overdue? Do you live by happenstance, because you want to avoid prioritizing? Do you automatically tackle the most complicated thing first to get it out of the way, or do you do the easy thing first to ease in to the hard stuff? How do you determine what gets your attention? Do you shuffle papers around on your desk until a dog-eared sheet catches your interest? Do you wait until your computer alerts you with a recurring ding that a deadline is fast approaching? Do you bow to the worthy agenda of an articulate family member, friend, boss, or coworker? Do you prioritize out of obligation, passion, or fear? Do you take time regularly to review God's priorities for your life? Do you have an accountability partner who helps you make periodic objective assessments of your roles and goals? Lisa Ryan, host of *The 700 Club*, admits that she has faced an ongoing struggle in this area.

## LISA RYAN HAD TO DEVISE SAFEGUARDS TO KEEP HER PRIORITIES IN CHECK

Lisa works out of the Christian Broadcast Network's (CBN's) Tennessee studios. She also enjoys speaking to girls and young women on some of the books she has authored: *For Such a Time as This* and *Generation Esther*. But Lisa cuts to the chase when she says that none of this would have any value if she were to neglect the four most important people in her life— her husband and three up-'n'-coming, modern-day Esthers (her daughters)!

Lisa prayed to receive Christ as her Savior at age five with her mother by her side. Since then, she has always had a deep hunger for God and has felt a sense of purpose and destiny. Her faith and trust in God have carried her through many difficult times, during which God continues to build her character and fill her with compassion for others. Through television, Lisa seeks to create a hunger for God and the abundant life he offers. Through writing and speaking, she gets to unleash her passion to challenge girls and young women to walk boldly and purposefully each day "for such a time as this" (as Esther's cousin said to her!).

Lisa prays constantly for God's direction in her life and for his help in prioritizing her roles and goals. In addition, she confesses that she is an endless list maker who feels enormous satisfaction when she crosses items off. Lisa also relies on her Palm Pilot and on her husband, who is a great balancer in her life on all levels—family, career, personal, and spiritual. When her schedule roars out of control and she starts feeling a little crazy, she stops, reevaluates, and eliminates. Then, she surrenders what's left undone to God and focuses her energies once again.

She says, "Prioritizing is a constant task that, if done well, will keep you from getting overwhelmed. But, if you don't prioritize using God's Spirit and his Word as your plumb line, you will lose your peace, feel like a failure, and end up doing nothing well. And that is never God's purpose. Beware of the *shoulds* other people assign to your life and learn to say no. Remember: Just because you *can*, doesn't mean you *have to*."

## How Do You Prioritize Your Roles and Goals?

## God Prioritized Well

God prioritized the roles and goals of the Israelites as he directed each step of their escape from the Egyptians: "By day the pillar of cloud did not cease to guide them [the Israelites] on their path, nor the pillar of fire by night to shine on the way they were to take" (Nehemiah 9:19). Please read the verse again. Picture God doing the same thing for you, day in and day out. How would you like that?

---

### SCRIPTURE TO PONDER

*Trust God from the bottom of your heart; don't try to figure out everything on your own. Listen for God's voice in everything you do, everywhere you go; he's the one who will keep you on track.*
*(Proverbs 3:5–6, MSG)*

## SUGGESTED PRAYER

*Dear Lord God, I, _____, trust you from the bottom of my heart, and I don't want to try to figure out everything on my own. I will listen for your voice in everything I do and everywhere I go. You're the one who will keep me on track. I acknowledge that it's your pathway, your map, and your speed limit! Today I pray that I will be a woman who seeks to know your priorities for my roles and goals. Help me balance my family and ministry life, my spirituality, and other pressing obligations. Guide me straight to your best for my life. Be clear with me, because I earnestly seek to honor you in all I do.*

**So . . . What Insight, Prayer, or Action Step Has God Laid on Your Heart Today?**

# In What Circumstance Has God Been Faithful to You?

According to John 14:2, Jesus has reserved a place for you in his Father's house. That is comforting news, but now think of a time when God has been faithful to you right here on earth, when he has opened the floodgates of his love. Your memory of it may involve a time when he drew you closer to him, created a miracle for you, gave you hope, guided you, or forgave you. Let today remind you that the height, depth, breadth, and length of God's faithfulness is immeasurable. Let it confirm to you that he will be faithful to tell you what he has in mind for your life's most extreme contribution!

## Let Me Count the Ways That God Is Faithful

Has God stayed by your side during an injustice? Was he faithful to watch over you during your college partying days, messy divorce, or depression? Did he minister to you throughout a long illness, forgive your rebelliousness, or reward you for your obedience? He is with you when your heart is breaking, your energy is sapped, and your hopes are dashed. He is faithful during trials, temptations, and learning curves. He is faithful in all circumstances, because he created you and loves you. Linda Evans Shepherd, host of the nationally syndicated radio show, *Right to the Heart*, has experienced God's faithfulness in very tangible ways.

## LINDA EVANS SHEPHERD TRUSTS ALMIGHTY GOD

Linda is an international speaker and author of fifteen books, including *Intimate Moments with God*, which is about women's changed lives. She also has authored several children's books. She is the founder of AWSA (Advanced Writers and Speakers Association) and founder and president of Right to the Heart Ministries, which regularly hosts conferences and publishes an e-magazine for women leaders and the women they lead. Linda continually looks for ways to grow deeper in her faith, joy, and leadership traits. She has been affirmed as a leader and encourager to Christian women leaders around the world.

God has been extremely faithful to Linda. When her infant daughter was profoundly disabled in a car accident a year before her son was born, Linda was a brokenhearted mother. But even in her deepest season of pain, she could sense that the Lord was gifting her with wisdom. Today, her children are teenagers, and she is in a new season of life. God is using Linda in ways she never would have imagined, especially in mentoring other women—which takes a whole lot of wisdom! Linda says, "Wait on the Lord. He will not only heal you, empower you, affirm you, and provide for you, he will also prepare you for the purpose of ministering mercy to others."

**In What Circumstance Has God Been Faithful to You?**

<br>

**Joshua Knew God Would Be Faithful**

Had Joshua not trusted God's faithfulness, he never could have marched the Israelites around the walled city of Jericho blowing trumpets as God had instructed him to do. Read Joshua 6:1–20. When have you felt God faithfully leading you with specific instructions?

## SCRIPTURE TO PONDER

*He is the Rock, his works are perfect, and all his ways are just.*
*A faithful God who does no wrong, upright and just is he.*
*(Deuteronomy 32:4)*

## SUGGESTED PRAYER

*Dear Lord, you are my Rock. Your works are perfect, and all your ways are just. You are a faithful God who does no wrong; upright and just are you. You have saved me and started me on the road to maturity. Today I, _____, humbly bow to thank you for your consistent faithfulness. You have never left my side. I ask you to let your grace and mercy flow into me daily, because I cannot live without your kindness. I pray that I will never take your continued faithfulness for granted, and that my awe of you will be a powerful testimony for all to hear.*

## So . . . What Insight, Prayer, or Action Step Has God Laid on Your Heart Today?

# Starting Today, How Can You Better Prepare for God's Purpose for Your Life?

Should there be any question about our willingness to prepare for our current or later-in-life mission? But being the mere humans that we are, some of us duck and dart and avoid the topic as if we are playing a game of dodgeball. It's important to remember that God knows every detail of the beginning, middle, and end of your story. He knows you intimately, and he can be fully trusted to prompt you about the next step to take. Have you asked him lately what you can do to prepare for his unique purpose for your life, especially for your later years when you may have more discretionary time? Just remember the old saying: "Be careful what you ask for. You just might get it!" What if you asked him to tell you what your next step should be, and he did! Would you do it? Would you, in preparation for greater assignments to come, do what he asked of you today?

## To Prepare or Not to Prepare?

In what way is God asking you to prepare for his plan for your life? Does he want you to get an accountability partner, listen to a wise counselor, save money regularly, or join a brand-new ministry? Does he want you to take a Bible class or keep a written record of your spiritual journey? What if he told you to practice perseverance, humility, or mercy? Do you think he wants you to take on a leadership role, be more grateful, believe that your life matters enormously to him, or show up in a difficult place where he is already at work? Mary Lance Sisk, author of *The Macedonian Project* prayer journal, is preparing for her next assignment in a rather bold fashion.

## MARY LANCE SISK IS PREPARING FOR WHATEVER GOD ASKS OF HER

Mary Lance is married to her childhood sweetheart and has four children (one other is deceased) and nine grandchildren. She was brought up by parents who encouraged her to give back to her community. She wrote a prayer journal for missionaries serving in the former USSR, which is now being used by Campus Crusade for Christ. She has also written a book, *Love Your Neighbor as Yourself: Blessing Your Neighborhood through Love and Prayer.* She is honored to currently serve on the board of directors of Mission America, a ministry designed to mobilize Christian leaders and individual Christians to reach America for Jesus Christ.

Mary Lance accepted a relationship with Jesus at age thirty-eight and immediately began to spend time alone with him each day in prayer and meditation. She has a hunger and thirst to know God and to help others do the same. She enjoys mentoring younger women, especially in the classical disciplines of solitude, silence, prayer, and spiritual fasting.

Mary Lance prepares for God's dream for her life by regularly listening to him and learning to obey his Word and promptings. She prays and practices Psalm 37:5, "Commit your way to the LORD," because she knows that obedient commitment is the key to the fulfillment of God's mission.

She says, "The best preparation is a way of life that moves you toward holiness. For example, it is important to begin your day in prayer and to read God's Word with an attitude of listening. It is also helpful to keep a journal about what the Lord is saying to you, including the steps and results of your obedience. And it is wise to end your day by making sure that you are not harboring any sin in your heart."

### Starting Today, How Can You Better Prepare for God's Purpose for Your Life?

### The Foolish Virgins Weren't Prepared

Five foolish virgins were rejected by the bridegroom for not having enough oil for their lamps. Read the parable of the ten virgins in Matthew 25:1–13. Have you ever read this parable and thought to yourself: *How could these women not have been ready for the most important event of their lives?* How might this story apply to you?

## SCRIPTURE TO PONDER

*[Jesus said,] "I have brought you glory on earth by completing the work you gave me to do." (John 17:4)*

## SUGGESTED PRAYER

*Dear Lord, with all my heart, I, _____, want to be able to say that I have brought you glory on earth by completing the work you gave me to do. Today I pray that you will prepare me well for whatever new or ongoing assignment you have in mind for me. I am ready, willing, and able to follow your lead.*

### So . . . What Insight, Prayer, or Action Step Has God Laid on Your Heart Today?

# WHAT ARE YOU HAPPY ABOUT?
# WHAT BRINGS YOU JOY?

One of the biggest discoveries of a woman's life is learning to differentiate between the concepts of happiness and joy. Happiness is based on temporal and worldly things like national holidays, finding a great restaurant, straight A's on your kid's report card, a jog along the beach, or a 30-percent off shoe sale! Joy is different. It comes from having Jesus in your heart. Whereas happiness is like a slice of chocolate cake, joy is more like having the recipe. Happiness does have its place in your life. It's actually God's gift of human emotion. Let's face it, a little fun and frivolity help get you through many otherwise dreary days! But Jesus did not die on the cross to make sure that you were happy, but rather to ensure that you would have the joy of knowing and glorifying him. Today it is critical that you stop to recognize the difference between being temporarily happy and having the long-lasting joy of Jesus. Let this concept teach you more about God's will for your life.

## HAPPY DAYS AND A JOYOUS LIFE

What's better than going to a theme park with your friends, getting a bonus at work, strolling with your sweetheart and an ice cream cone, or taking a bubble bath by candlelight? "Not much!" you say? What about the satisfaction of a delicious home-cooked meal with family members or the delight of curling up by a fireplace to read a great book? It's all good! There's nothing better except to intentionally choose to add the deep joy of knowing Jesus and living a life devoted to him. LaVonna Floreal, an Olympic silver medal winner in the 100-meter hurdles, is beginning to fully appreciate the difference between life's everyday pleasures and the deeper bliss of knowing Jesus.

## LaVONNA FLOREAL PREFERS JOY

LaVonna is a wife and mother of two children, a fifth-grade teacher at a Christian school, and a two-time Olympian. LaVonna knows that she is a work-in-progress, engaged in the ongoing process of recognizing God's will in all aspects of her life. Even though she does not understand all that God is doing, she is learning how to choose joy in the journey. She says that she is not where she would like to be in many areas, but that she will continue to strive to know more about her heavenly Father.

LaVonna loves to encourage and train young people to set and reach their life goals, but only when she can maintain some resemblance to a Proverbs 31 woman-in-training. To her, that is a woman who aspires to do all she can in meeting the needs of her family. She focuses her mind, soul, and body on honoring the Lord by being a good wife and mother.

By the world's definition of happiness—having a great family and home, income, status, notoriety—LaVonna is happy. However, the daily challenges that life presents—relationships, children's schedules, and the "what if" worry games—cause her emotional barometer to bounce. So the Holy Spirit is teaching her to rely on him to live a joy-filled life centered on Jesus Christ and not on her ever-changing feelings of happiness and unhappiness.

LaVonna says, "I am slowly learning to give my concerns and worries to God, so they do not wreak havoc on my emotional stability. I want the Holy Spirit to help me mature emotionally. I believe that the secret to everlasting joy (instead of temporary happiness) is choosing to be content in Christ whatever his wishes, whatever the circumstances."

**What Are You Happy About? What Brings You Joy?**

### Mary of Bethany Sought Joy

Mary of Bethany sat at the feet of Jesus, listening to every word he said. She must have felt like she was in heaven. Read Luke 10:38–42. When do you most feel the joy of knowing Jesus?

## Scripture to Ponder

*I have learned the secret of being content in any and every situation, whether well fed or hungry, whether living in plenty or in want. I can do everything through him who gives me strength.*
*(Philippians 4:12-13)*

## Suggested Prayer

*Dear Lord Jesus, I, _____, want to learn more about the secret of being content in any and every situation, whether well fed or hungry, whether living in plenty or in want. I believe your Word when it tells me that I can do everything through you who give me strength. Today I pray that my days will be filled with the full measure of abundant joy that only you can give. Help me focus on you and on how much you love me, not on things that bring me fleeting happiness.*

### So . . . What Insight, Prayer, or Action Step Has God Laid on Your Heart Today?

# What Ingrained Belief Do You Need to Challenge?

What incorrect or ungodly belief was ingrained into you as a child? Do you understand that the first step in changing a long-held, mistaken belief is identifying it as false? Take that step today. Denounce it. Ask God to rid you of any diseased thinking. Tell him that you do not want your incorrect thinking to cause a delay in the unfolding of his plan for your life. Next, depending on how much credence you gave to a false belief over the years, you may need to write down what you *now* believe and why you believe it. Date the entry and review it periodically. Then, ask a good friend to hold you accountable to owning your new beliefs.

## Lies Will Be Exposed

Today is a good day to change incorrect concepts in your belief system. Were you taught that God is harsh or that you have to earn your salvation through good works? Is it time for any of these thoughts to change: *Don't trust anyone. I have to look out for my own best interest. Everything's relative and there are no absolutes, so I do whatever works for me. There are many ways to get into heaven, not just through Jesus. I'm a victim. I'm not good enough to help others. I'm not smart enough, holy enough, worthy enough, prepared enough, pretty enough, or articulate enough. Satan can snatch me out of God's hand if I sin,* which translates as *my salvation is not secure!* How many more years are you willing to listen to that type of deceitful thinking? Even one more day is too long. Christine Wyrtzen, founder of Daughters of Promise, eventually said, "Enough! I need to find the truth for myself," and she did.

## Christine Wyrtzen Is Free at Last

Christine is a recording artist, author, speaker, and host of the nationally syndicated radio program, *Daughters of Promise.* She has recorded fifteen albums and written two books. Christine says that the greatest thing she has learned in the past twenty years is that being a Christian woman means loving and being loved, not giving an impeccable performance. Christine believes that living out God's truth involves a spiritual transformation at the core of our being. She says that engaging in behavior modification techniques, which lead us to comply with a belief system for the sake of complying, is not helpful in discovering God's best for our lives. Christine feels called to awaken women to the extravagant love of God and teach them to live as much-loved daughters of the King.

Long ago, Christine decided: "The Bible is simply a textbook and, therefore, God is a subject to be studied." To her, the Bible only represented law, not life. Every verse was one more thing to add to her already exhaustive list of expectations. No more! She finally realized that couldn't possibly be correct. Where were the freedom and free will supposedly promised to

Christians? She finally mustered the courage to question her basic childhood beliefs. Now she exclaims to all that it's as if her soul was awakened out of a deep sleep. She embraces the love of God, as expressed through the exquisite beauty of his Word, and she has a profound sense of well-being. She knows that the Bible is the living, breathing revelation of God, designed to help us know him.

She says, "From time to time, it is important to stop and think about what you believe. Make a list of your core beliefs, and then pray about each one for a full day before you come to any final conclusions. It will amaze you how much incorrect thinking you are carrying around from your youth, when you were not spiritually mature enough to sort through concepts for yourself."

**What Ingrained Belief Do You Need to Challenge?**

**The Prodigal Son Changed His Belief**

The prodigal son believed that his father owed him his inheritance! He had a dangerous attitude of personal entitlement, until he had squandered his money and had to acknowledge his sin. Read Luke 15:11–32. What harmful belief has taken one of your loved ones down the wrong path?

## SCRIPTURE TO PONDER

*Your word is a lamp to my feet and a light for my path.*
*(Psalm 119:105)*

## SUGGESTED PRAYER

*Dear Lord, your Word is a lamp to my feet and a light for my path. Today I, _____, pray that you would shake up my thinking and help me challenge my ingrained beliefs. Walk alongside me as I dare to uncover false doctrine, wrong theology, unfair opinions, debilitating comments, and ungodly teachings. Don't let these thoughts hold me captive any longer. I want you to release me to live the abundant life that you have planned for me.*

### So . . . What Insight, Prayer, or Action Step Has God Laid on Your Heart Today?

# WHAT DO YOU REGRET?

God is aware of all your regrets, and he wants you to admit them, learn from them, make restitution (if needed), and move on. He knows that your deepest regrets can become the best part of your testimony about his grace. Regardless of what you've done in the past, let today steer you away from a life of shame and into one of rejoicing in the chance to start over. If you stay focused on your regrets after having confessed them, repented of them, and been forgiven, you will miss the blessings God has planned for you. Put your regrets behind you, and make the contribution to this world that he reserved for you to make.

## REGRETS BEGET REGRETS

People commonly regret that they did not forgive someone before he or she died, or that they did not tell that person about Jesus. Has that happened to you, or is your biggest regret more centered around an incident of poor parenting or that you ignored a friend's cry for help? Some women regret a lie they told or a time they cheated or stole. What behavior has caused regret in your life? A moral failure, abandoned dreams, cowardly behavior, a spiteful act, or boasting? Was it that you were too busy to enjoy family outings, made a poor decision based on insufficient information, hurt someone out of jealousy, were stubborn, or blamed someone else for your mistake? Did you participate in a cover-up, get fired for not being honest, or give in to sinful peer pressure? Is your biggest regret that you have not forgiven yourself or that you have lived with anger for too long? Which of your regrets actually begot another regret? Lisa Smith-Batchen, a multi-sport, adventure-racer and one of the world's top ultra-distance, endurance athletes, had an unusual regret that gave her a second chance to make it right.

## LISA SMITH-BATCHEN GIVES HER REGRETS TO GOD

Lisa holds a master's degree in health education and fitness; she has been a personal trainer, coach, and massage therapist for more than fifteen years. She and her husband are the proud parents of two children, whom they adopted within six months of each other. One of her favorite endeavors is motivational speaking on the topic of "Find a Godly Dream and Chase It Down." Anyone would tell you that Lisa is an incredibly loving and compassionate woman, who seeks to please God in all she does.

God has enabled Lisa to challenge her mind, body, and soul to race hundreds of miles each year, while in the process raising money to feed thousands of starving children. She plans to continue to do so as long as God wills it, because she wants to inspire others to have Mother Teresa–sized dreams to save the children of the world.

Because Lisa believes in finishing what she starts, she regretted not completing one particular journey she started, that is, running three hundred miles through California's Death Valley. So, one blistering hot summer, Lisa set out on what she called her "journey of completion." As she crossed the finish line, she put the regret behind her.

She says, "What you decide to do with your regrets is the ultimate test of your character. Rebounding from regrets will make you a woman of godly character. There is no regret in your life that God cannot turn into a gift and a growth experience. It's reflecting on the setbacks in life that makes you see how far you've really come."

## What Do You Regret?

## Judas Regretted His Sin

Judas had the greatest regret known to man; that is, betraying the Son of God. Because of that sin, Judas hung himself. Read Matthew 27:1–10. Each one of us, by our own sins, also betrayed Jesus and caused his crucifixion. What percentage of time do you live a life filled with various regrets—big or small—rather than living the redeemed life that Christ intended?

## SCRIPTURE TO PONDER

*You don't want to end your life full of regrets, nothing but sin and bones, saying, "Oh, why didn't I do what they told me? Why did I reject a disciplined life? Why didn't I listen to my mentors, or take my teachers seriously? My life is ruined! I haven't one blessed thing to show for my life!"*
(Proverbs 5:11 – 14, MSG)

## SUGGESTED PRAYER

*Dear Lord, I, _____, don't want to end my life full of regrets, nothing but sin and bones, saying, "Oh, why didn't I do what wise instructors told me? Why did I reject a disciplined life? Why didn't I listen to my mentors, or take my teachers seriously? My life is ruined! I haven't one blessed thing to show for my life!" Today I pray that I will chase down my godly dream, so I will not live in regret that I missed the opportunity to do so. Take my regrets—all of them—and restore my life with a clean slate. Thank you that you allow me to start over again and again and again.*

## So . . . What Insight, Prayer, or Action Step Has God Laid on Your Heart Today?

# What Is Your Greatest Hope or Deepest Longing?

Many women have trouble focusing on their greatest hopes and deepest longings. Some feel they don't deserve the incredible gift; others are too tired to care about such unrealistic loftiness; still others refuse to verbalize their wish for fear of it coming true and changing their life. Pause for a moment to remember who put hopes and longings in your soul. God did! Acknowledge him and thank him for his love. What do you hope for or long for that, perhaps, you've never told another living soul before? What would, absolutely, be too great a gift to you? What would cause you to shake your head in disbelief and live in gratitude? Pray persistently until your miracle arrives, and in the meantime, do your part with utmost faithfulness. Make this exercise today a prayer to God about your hopes and longings. If you honestly can't think of anything that you long for right now, just smile and pray in full anticipation that you will soon discover or rediscover it! God wired you to have hopes and longings.

## WHAT WOULD ROCK YOUR WORLD?

For a moment, try to ignore all possible excuses for not being able to dream. Do you wish you could live in a house with a white picket fence, see the world, gain or lose weight, explore the arts, or run a marathon? Do you hope to take piano lessons, learn sign language, or regain your health? Do you pray diligently about having a child, finding a book agent, or becoming a career missionary? Do you want to get married, take a sabbatical, or get out of debt? Do you long to hear your unique assignment in God's "glory story," use more of your giftedness in your career, or see your daughter marry a loving, Christian man who would be the spiritual leader of their household? Remember, dreams do come true! Let Nancy Stafford, who played Andy Griffith's law partner for five years on the television show, *Matlock*, share one of her greatest hopes with you.

## NANCY STAFFORD HAS SEEN DREAMS COME TRUE

Nancy has been a costar on numerous television series and movies. Host of TV's *Main Floor* for the past nine years, she also has authored two books: *The Wonder of His Love: A Journey into the Heart of God* and *Beauty by the Book: Seeing Yourself as God Sees You.* As a speaker and author, she sets out to lead others toward freedom and wholeness. She loves helping them realize their true identity and worth, and thus grasp the depth of God's great love for them.

Nancy has a passion for quieting her soul and pursuing intimacy with God. She and her husband, Larry Myers, a pastor and worship leader, operate their ranch retreat center in Southern California where people can go to restore and refresh their souls and to work on creative projects.

Nancy says that one of her greatest hopes is that she will continue to be used by God to help others get their dreams out of their hearts and into reality. She says that this often happens with prayer, reflection, and Holy Spirit–led conversations in the peaceful ranch setting. Nancy longs to develop a more intentional mentoring process to help people devote their lives to Christ and his plans.

She says, "God has given each of us a dream—a treasure—as an aspect of his own heart. To discover the gift that he's placed in your heart, ask yourself, 'What burdens me?' and 'What am I hungering for?' And don't forget to help others along the way—because as we help others fulfill their godly dreams and vision, we begin to see more clearly the dream God has placed in our own heart."

## What Is Your Greatest Hope or Deepest Longing?

## King David Had a Longing

King David, the Levites, and the people of Israel dreamed of bringing the ark of the Lord's covenant to Jerusalem. It had been in Baalah for twenty years. Read 1 Chronicles 15:1–16:3. Do you feel like you have been waiting forever (five, ten, twenty years) for your longing to come to fruition? If yes, how are you holding up?

## Scripture to Ponder

*All my longings lie open before you, O Lord;*
*my sighing is not hidden from you. (Psalm 38:9)*

## Suggested Prayer

*O dear Lord, all my longings lie open before you; my sighing is*
*not hidden from you. Today I, _____, pray that you will*
*grant me or inspire in me a great hope, a deep longing. Help*
*me not feel selfish or guilty for wanting to have and become all*
*you desire. At the same time, I surrender to you even my present*
*and future longings and your providential intervention in*
*making them come true. I put each day in your capable hands.*

### So . . . What Insight, Prayer, or Action Step Has God Laid on Your Heart Today?

# What Have You Learned from One of Your Failures?

You can't escape failure. It can crop up in your vocation, education, marriage, or parenting. It can be a moral failure, a sin of omission, or a case of poor judgment. What's the benefit of digging up an old failure and reliving that sadness? Why bother to recall an ethical, legal, financial, or relational problem? It's for one reason only: so you can record what, if anything, you learned from it. God is patient, but he is also lovingly persistent. He expects you to learn from your mistakes or to retake the test. So, what good thing have you learned from one of your failures? Remember that each failure you learn from will be one less failure you have to worry about during God's next purpose for your life.

## There's No Shortage of Failures

The value of a failure is in what you learn from it. For example, through a failure, did God teach you to consider others' feelings, to pray for wisdom, or to think before you speak? What was the takeaway from one of your failures? Did you learn to set appropriate boundaries, live in gratitude, stop judging others, or show kindness to those who hate you? Did you learn not to take shortcuts; that perfectionism can give you an ulcer; that what goes around comes around; or that God is faithful? Dottie McDowell, wife and helpmate of Josh at Campus Crusade for Christ, eventually decided to take bold measures to pass the test that she felt she had failed too many times.

## DOTTIE MCDOWELL GETS DO-OVERS

After becoming a Christian in her senior year of college, Dottie prayed that God would allow her to marry a man who wanted to make an impact for Christ around the world. The Lord directly answered that prayer. She soon met and married her husband Josh, who became an international author and lecturer with Campus Crusade for Christ. It is her joy and privilege to help Josh reach people with the gospel message.

In the front of Dottie's Bible, she has written these words: "The most important thing I can do in life is to take God's Word seriously." Her fervent prayer is that she will be faithful to this challenge and that she will help others to do the same. She says she is blessed to have been raised by a loving mother who constantly told her what a delight and honor it is to be a mom. God used her mother's life to instill in Dottie a desire to be a mom who trusts the Lord. She believes that God, in turn, has called her to encourage others—especially mothers—to trust him and to delight in the children he has given them.

Dottie recalls one of her repeated failures: "I sometimes sent one or more of my children off to school with an unkind word or attitude. I learned that I could do something about this particular failure. I made a vow that if I acted in this way, I'd stuff my pockets with candy kisses, drive right over to the school, get the child out of class, apologize—and then share the candy kisses!" She adds, "Always ask God for a chance to start over. He is a God of second chances—and third, and fourth, and fifth!"

## What Have You Learned from One of Your Failures?

### Peter Failed

Peter denied knowing Jesus three times. Later, Jesus gave Peter a chance to accept him three times. Peter did, and then went on to serve and lead others. Read Mark 14:66–72 and John 21:15–19. If Jesus reached out to Peter with abundant love after Peter had failed him so brashly, don't you think the Savior of the world will do the same for you when you fail?

## SCRIPTURE TO PONDER

*No, dear brothers and sisters, I am still not all I should be,*
*but I am focusing all my energies on this one thing:*
*Forgetting the past and looking forward to what lies ahead,*
*I strain to reach the end of the race and receive the prize*
*for which God, through Christ Jesus, is calling us up to heaven.*
*(Philippians 3:13-14, NLT)*

## SUGGESTED PRAYER

*Dear Lord, I, _____, admit to you and to my dear
brothers and sisters that I am still not all I should be, but I am
focusing all my energies on this one thing: Forgetting the past
and looking forward to what lies ahead, I strain to reach the
end of the race and receive the prize for which God, through
Christ Jesus, is calling me up to heaven. Today I thank you for
forgiving me for all my failures! I ask you to stay by my side,
as I learn from my next mistakes.*

### So . . . What Insight, Prayer, or Action Step Has God Laid on Your Heart Today?

# WHAT IN YOUR LIFE NEEDS FURTHER CLARIFICATION?

When you clarify something, you illuminate it or shed light on it. Ask yourself today: "What area of my life *still* needs a floodlight shined on it?" There's so much to figure out and so little time to do it, that you even need to be clear about what you need clarified! In other words, ask God specifically what you want to know. Learning to ask for clarity is a skill that will help you become all God intends for you to become.

## HELP, I NEED CLARITY!

Are you still having trouble trying to decide where to worship on Sundays or what school to choose? Do you need help clarifying what house rules to set for teenagers, how to help a friend who is a hypochondriac, or how to find a spiritual growth mentor? Do you need clarification about whether to ask a secular expert or a Christian counselor for advice, what cause to champion, what rights to give up, what goals to set, how to find a job that uses your passion and spiritual gifts, or how to establish a budget? Are your supervisor's instructions still unclear to you, or do you need more information about a health issue? Becky Tirabassi has sold more than a million books, tapes, and videos, including *Change Your Life*, but she is ready for God to clarify one important assignment.

## BECKY TIRABASSI VALUES CLARITY

Becky is president of Becky Tirabassi Change Your Life® Inc., a multimedia (television, radio, and publishing) company designed to encourage people to change their lives for the better—physically, emotionally, spiritually, and mentally. She has been married for more than twenty-five years and is the mother of an adult son.

Two decades ago, Becky made a commitment to God to pray for an extended time each day, and she is humbled that he has helped her keep that commitment. She believes that these appointments with God have singlehandedly changed every area of her life, and that they will continue to do so! Becky shares that, from the moment of her dramatic conversion to Christ at age twenty-one, lifting her from alcoholism and immorality, she was compelled to share the love, forgiveness, and power of the living, loving God with anyone who would listen. She was drawn especially to those who were seeking love, hope, and truth, but who were not going to a church to find the answers. After a forty-day partial fast eight years ago, she felt God directing her to start a company designed to creatively reach unbelievers with a balanced-life message. Today, this company is helping millions of Christians and those seeking Christ.

Becky isn't timid about asking what next steps she needs clarified to pursue her own television talk show. She comments that she feels similar to how Joshua probably felt standing at the edge of the Jordan River before crossing over. She knows that she must take a step of faith, believing God to do the impossible, yet the outcome is ominous unless God intervenes to open doors. On the tough days, when nothing but rejection calls come in, it's easy to wonder if she heard God correctly. But fueled by faith, tenacity, and her husband's encouragement, she is compelled by the dream God put in her heart many years ago that will not go away: to take the good news to those who need him, don't know him, and have misconceptions about him and Christians.

She says, "My greatest resource for ongoing clarification has been the prayer journal, *My Partner*, God prompted me to design. If I did not write down that I regularly hear him telling me to *keep coming*, the disappointments would have caused me to give up long ago. But because God makes just enough time in my schedule each day for me to read from my 365-day Bible and then journal, there is one voice I continue to hear above all others."

### What in Your Life Needs Further Clarification?

### Martha Needed Clarification

Martha needed to understand the value of *being* versus *doing*, to realize that sitting at Jesus' feet, like her sister Mary, was just as vital as preparing the evening meal. Read Luke 10:38–42. Is the balance between being and doing something you need clarified?

## SCRIPTURE TO PONDER

*"I [God] speak to him [Moses] face to face, directly and not in riddles! He sees the LORD as he is." (Numbers 12:8, NLT)*

## SUGGESTED PRAYER

*Dear Lord God, speak to me, _____, face to face, directly and not in riddles! I want to hear your voice clearly and see you as you are. Today I pray for clarification from you about all aspects of my life and about my next steps, every step of the way. I ask for my eyes to be opened as you allow me to see the truth you want me to see. Take away all of my deliberate, spiritual blindness.*

## So . . . What Insight, Prayer, or Action Step Has God Laid on Your Heart Today?

# Special Instructions for Day 60

Today is the final day of guided prayer about your life
purposes. (In Part 2 you will analyze what you have
discovered while praying.) For this Day 60 exercise,
your role is going to be dramatically different. You
are going to be the influential woman who others look
up to. To start off, I want you to imagine that it is
five, ten, or twenty years from now—however much
time you think you are going to need to become
incredibly influential! After you have read all the
instructions, you can indicate in the spaces provided
what year you'd like it to be and what corresponding
age that would make you.

The Year _____     Your Age _____

Now, imagine that you are living in that projected
future year. And, imagine that I have heard that you
are a highly respected, godly woman of great influence in Christian circles. In fact, I have just sent you
the following interview form, inviting you to be part

of my soon-to-be-released book that helps women pray about their life purposes. Play along here and say yes to my invitation to be interviewed by me!

Next, imagine that many women readers will be reading what you submit to me for publication. That means your description of your personal life, your spirituality, and your life mission, as well as your answer to today's primary question, "What's Your Motive?" will be a learning guide for others. So far, so good?

Please answer the seven Day 60 introductory questions and primary question *as if* you already are the incredibly influential, Christian woman that God intends you to be, whether you have ever felt significantly used by him or not. Today is about helping you see yourself and your future through God's eyes. Please dream more boldly and purposefully than you have ever allowed yourself to do before, without letting any hint of judgment or criticism creep in from yourself or anyone else.

I want you to have fun with this exercise! Breathe, relax, enjoy, and prayerfully surrender all your preconceived ideas about who you are and what God's purposes are for your life. Be prepared to capture in your futurist profile those things that are impossible for you, but oh so possible for God. Focus on the King of kings, not on your smallness. Focus on the Lord of all, who has the resources to give you the godly desires of your heart. Focus on your heavenly Father, who actually put those desires in your heart.

Start by reading through the entire Day 60 exercise, so you will know more specifically where this assignment is headed. Then, be still for a while, sitting in the presence of your Savior. (If you have not made Christ your Savior, turn to page 300 and prayerfully consider doing so now.)

Next, ask God to reveal powerful answers to you today. Expect him to talk to you about things he planned for you before you were ever born! Tell him that you promise to be a good listener.

Then, quickly answer all seven questions before you have a chance to sabotage this exercise. How could you sabotage it? You might begin to doubt that it is the Holy Spirit prompting your answers; you might panic or be embarrassed about the bigness of what you see yourself writing; you might allow Satan to convince you that you are acting puffed up and prideful; or you might allow yourself to be distracted, just to name a few ways! Your uninhibited responses will give you some final valuable insight that you will need in Part 2.

By the way, if you need some hints about how to answer any of your Day 60 questions, just look back over Days 1–59 to recall how other influential women have responded to their similar questions. There are no right or wrong, cookie-cutter answers. Just go with the flow of the Holy Spirit's inspiration.

Today is all about God's boldest plan for you. Let this be a life-changing experience that moves you light-years ahead on your pathway to purpose!

# WHAT'S YOUR MOTIVE FOR SERVING?

*Remember, you are the influential woman today! I'll take over the parts you've typically been doing on Days 1-59, so don't worry about those. Just have fun being influential.*

What is your real underlying motive for much of the apparently good stuff you do? It's amazing how often there is a huge disparity between our impure motives and the supposed goodness of our actions. Think about it. Things are not always what they seem. Is there sometimes a gaping chasm between how you *really* feel versus how you pretend to feel? Bottom line: only God and you know for sure! It is important to purify your motives, before you ask your Lord to reveal your next purpose-in-life.

## NOW THERE'S AN INTERESTING MOTIVE!

When you serve, are you really trying to impress someone with your talent, beauty, or knowledge? Do you serve to mask your pain or boredom, to satisfy your curiosity, or to relieve your guilt? When you give generously, are you actually trying to enhance your reputation or be forgiven? Do you do things just to feel good or get a thrill? Do you go to church to fulfill your obligation? Do you get involved to manipulate a response or take advantage of someone? In reality, is it to get a reaction, pity, recognition, or money? Do you volunteer in your child's classroom primarily to critique the new teacher or ward off loneliness? Do you share prayer requests for a chance to gossip?

Or, is your agenda to give glory to God? Is it to represent Jesus to someone by serving him or her? Is it to spread the good news of the gospel or to ask for God's help? Listen to what this influential woman has to say about her motives.

1. What's your first and last name?

_____

2. What is a general, one-sentence description of yourself as God sees you—as a godly, influential woman?

_____

_____

3. How would you describe your personal life? (This section is about who you are, *as if* it already were how you and God wanted it to be. There are *no* right or wrong topics to include in this introductory section; however, save comments about your "spirituality" and "reason you were born" for questions 4 and 5.)

_____

_____

_____

4. How would you describe your spirituality, *as if* it already were how you and God wanted it to be?

5. How would you describe why you were born, *as if* you were living the life you were meant to live? This is where you should talk boldly about what God has asked you to do or about your unique life purpose, *as if* it has already happened! It should be more specific than your personal or spiritual answers above. Write a GOD-SIZED response overflowing with his best design for your life!

6. How would you answer today's question: "What's Your Motive for Serving?"

7. Will you write a two-sentence quote, as a woman of influence, to give some clarity or hope or advice to others about the importance of having pure motives?

 

## What's Your Motive?
   *Katie's Answer:*

To answer that question, I have to ask you what day of the week it is—because that's about how often my motives change. For the most part, my motives for serving others are because God is my God and he has commanded me to love others, forgive them, wash their feet, point them to Jesus, disciple them, and worship with them. I serve to obey God and bring him glory. I serve because my heart breaks over the evil in this world. I want to be a change agent who helps people know the power, mercy, and grace of God. So, that's how I'm feeling today. Other days I serve to impress people, to be thanked, to feel good about my contribution, or to relieve my guilt. I think the one impure motive that disgusts me the most is when I serve to try to get attention.

## Samuel Learned about Motives

When Samuel anointed David king over Israel, the Lord told Samuel not to look at David's outward appearance, because he, the Lord, looks at the heart. Read 1 Samuel 16:1–13. Are you any good at reading other people's hidden motives?

*Katie's Answer:*

Yes, I would say that I am. Probably because I've got so many hidden ones myself, I've become quite good at spotting hypocrisy!

## SCRIPTURE TO PONDER

*We justify our actions by appearances;*
*GOD examines our motives. (Proverbs 21:2, MSG)*

## SUGGESTED PRAYER

*Dear Lord God, help me, [Katie], not to be self-deceived, not to justify my actions because, on the surface, they appear good. Instead, teach me to examine my motives like you do. Today I pray that I will see my wrong motives in your crystal-clear light. Forgive me for all the times I have acted out of impure motives. And, thank you that you have helped me to have right motives in your sight many times. Convict me daily with the acid test: "Are my motives pleasing to you, God?"*

### So . . . What Insight, Prayer, or Action Step Has God Laid on Your Heart Today?

*Katie's Answer:*

Today, I will ask my ministry partner if she would like to go to lunch on Sunday at noon or sometime within the next two weeks. At lunch, I will ask her if she will be my accountability partner in this area of pure and impure motives. I will give her permission to ask me about my motives for any and all assignments and relationships, and I will promise her a blunt response each time she asks.

Part Two

# *Inviting the* Holy Spirit *to Reveal Your Life* Purposes

Now that you have prayed for sixty days about your life purposes, invite the Holy Spirit to help you draw whatever conclusions he is ready for you to see.

# Classifying Your Responses

This exercise categorizes what you have learned about yourself and about God's call on your life thus far. To fill in the information requested on the following pages, turn first to each specified "question-of-the-day" in Part 1 (the page number is provided in parentheses for your convenience). Review those answers. In abbreviated form (four to eight words) fill them in below. This will ensure that you recap the highlights of your prayer-filled journey-to-purpose in a summary format.

For example:

## Things Potentially Blocking Your Life Purpose

**Day 1:** What are you afraid of?

Rejection, dogs, lightning,

giving speeches

## God's Ingredients for Your Life Purpose

**Day 6:** What are a few of your talents or skills?

Playing piano, gardening,

snow skiing, researching

If you previously skipped any answer, try to answer it at this time. Plan to spend thirty minutes doing this transcription exercise.

## THINGS POTENTIALLY BLOCKING YOUR LIFE PURPOSE

**Day 1:** What are you afraid of? (page 31)


**Day 11:** How do you self-sabotage? (page 71)


**Day 12b:** What's wrong in your life? (page 75)


**Day 14:** What roadblocks have you encountered in your life? (page 83)


**Day 24:** What do you need to confess? (page 124)


**Day 36:** What is your unhealthy method of escape? (page 172)

**Day 40:** What is the root cause of your anger? (page 188)

**Day 42:** What do you need to surrender? (page 196)

**Day 43:** How do you try to steal God's glory? (page 199)

**Day 45:** What is your prized excuse? (page 208)

## THINGS CONFUSING YOU IN LIFE

**Day 4:** What's confused in your life? (page 43)

**Day 26:** What would you like to change about yourself? (page 132)

**Day 48:** What baggage are you carrying that you don't want? (page 221)

**Day 50:** What current activity or opportunity might be a distraction? (page 229)

**Day 59:** What in your life needs further clarification? (page 266)

## GOD'S INGREDIENTS FOR YOUR LIFE PURPOSE

**Day 6:** What are a few of your talents or skills? (page 51)

**Day 10:** What are two of your best personal qualities? (page 66)

**Day 33:** What weakness of yours has God turned into a strength? (page 160)

**Day 47:** What are your spiritual gifts? (page 216)

**Day 54:** What are you happy about? What brings you joy? (page 246)

## METHODS AND PROCESSES FOR DISCOVERING YOUR LIFE PURPOSE

**Day 23:** What's going on in your quiet time with the Lord? (page 120)

**Day 39:** How does God get through to you? (page 184)

## FACETS OF YOUR MOST UNIQUE LIFE PURPOSE

**Day 15:** What are your hobbies? (page 87)

**Day 17:** What were you born to tell the world? (page 95)

**Day 19:** What has been your favorite job, ministry, or community volunteer opportunity? (page 103)

**Day 21:** Weighing everything, what do you want out of life? (page 112)

**Day 29:** Other than God and your family, what do you value most?
(page 144)

**Day 32:** What do you want to be doing for God ten years from now?
(page 156)

**Day 41:** How would you spend your last week on earth? (page 192)

**Day 49:** To whom has God called you? (page 225)

**Day 57:** What is your greatest hope or deepest longing? (page 258)

## HISTORICAL CLUES ABOUT YOUR FUTURE LIFE PURPOSES

**Day 2:** What consequences have you faced from a life mistake? (page 35)

**Day 5:** How did God use a crisis or problem to bring good into your life? (page 47)

**Day 8:** Who is your hero or role model? (page 59)

**Day 13:** What was a turning point in your life? (page 79)

**Day 25:** Where have you searched for significance? (page 127)

## Factors Affecting Your Receptivity of Life Purpose

**Day 7:** How do you define success? (page 54)


**Day 12a:** What's right in your life? (page 75)


**Day 28:** Where is your current mission field? (page 140)


**Day 31:** What's missing in your life? (page 151)


**Day 35:** What do you need to learn? (page 168)


**Day 56:** What do you regret? (page 254)

**Day 58:** What have you learned from one of your failures? (page 262)

**Day 60:** What's your motive for serving? (page 273)
(Use your "influential woman" answer!)

## Absolute Necessities for Living Out Your Life Purpose

**Day 3:** When have you persevered? (page 39)

**Day 34:** How balanced is your life? (page 164)

**Day 44:** How often and how hard do you laugh? (page 204)

**Day 46:** What are you most grateful for? (page 211)

## God's Equipping for Your Life Purpose

**Day 9:** What comment or conversation has had a great impact on you? (page 63)

**Day 16:** Who is in your professional, ministerial, or emotional network? (page 91)

**Day 27:** When have you taken a quantum leap of faith? (page 136)

**Day 30:** What equipping do you still need for God's work? (page 148)

**Day 37:** When have you obeyed God? (page 176)

**Day 51:** How do you prioritize your roles and goals? (page 233)

**Day 53:** Starting today, how can you better prepare for God's purpose for your life? (page 242)

## SPECIFIC AREAS YOU NEED TO GROW IN TO SUPPORT YOUR LIFE PURPOSE

**Day 18:** How is God developing your character? (page 99)

**Day 22:** What strength of yours can easily become a weakness? (page 116)

**Day 55:** What ingrained belief do you need to challenge? (page 250)

## What You Know about God Almighty, Who Gives Purpose to Your Life

**Day 20:** In what situation was God's power evident to you? (page 107)

**Day 38:** When have you experienced God's timing in your life? (page 180)

**Day 52:** In what circumstance has God been faithful to you? (page 238)

Before going further, slowly and prayerfully reread each of your answers in this exercise. Attempt to digest them as a unit of information. Then, use this summary chart to help you answer most of the questions in the next exercises.

# DISCOVERING YOUR LIFE THEMES, PATTERNS, AND ACTION STEPS

Answer all the questions in this section on pages 291–296. Trust the Holy Spirit to guide your thoughts. Ask him to remove all spiritual blinders and lead you to truth. To do this exercise, you will need to refer back to the answers you just transcribed on pages 280–290 in "Classifying Your Responses."

1. Which two to three answers bothered you the most (i.e., confused you, made you angry, or were difficult)? Why?

2. Which two to three answers pleasantly surprised you (i.e., came easily to you, were affirming, or helped you see a pattern)? Why?

3. Considering all your answers, what two to three things did you notice about yourself that you would like to change? Why?

4. What have been one or two themes of your life? (*I'm no good. I can't. Life is unfair. Day late and a dollar short. I refuse to be a victim. I can do all things through him who gives me strength. Life is a glorious adventure.*)

Do you want those themes to continue in your life? Why or why not?

5. What two to three patterns do you see in your answers (i.e., rebellion, regrets, broken promises, anger, fear, sabotage, lost dreams, joy, friendships, hope, vision)?

How do those patterns make you feel? Why?

6. Which two to three answers shed light on your past, present, or future assignment(s) from God? In what ways are they helpful?

7. From what you notice—even if they don't seem logical to you right now—what appear to be your current life purposes?

From what you notice—even if it doesn't seem logical to you right now—what appears to be your most unique, later-in-life purpose (beyond the years you'll devote to education, marriage, childrearing, and/or career positioning)?

8. Take some time to prayerfully reread all of your "Insights, Prayers, and Action Steps" from Days 1–59. In light of your self-analysis in Part 2, which five action steps are the most important ones for you to take within the next one to five months? Write five steps you would like to take:

By _____ , I will

By _____ , I will

By _____ , I will

By _____ , I will _____

By _____ , I will _____

Are you committed to taking these five steps within the next one to five months? If yes, why? If no, why not?

_____

_____

_____

_____

_____

## FUTURE ACTION STEPS

The first time I read and prayed through this book was:

From _____ to _____

Other times that I read and prayed these topics and chose action steps:

From _____ to _____

From _____ to _____

From _____ to _____

# My Journal Notes
## Of _____'s Insights

Now it's time to meet with a trusted family member or female friend, making sure to carefully explain the reason for your meeting, which is to help you process your conclusions and action steps. (It is fine for an unmarried woman to meet with an unmarried man.) To invite the peson into a conversation, you may want to say: "I'd like to chat with you about a prayerful self-analysis I just did regarding my life purposes. I'd particularly love to get your input about my life themes, patterns, and next action steps, based on what I believe my life purposes are."

When you meet, ask him/her to take a look at your answers for "Classifying Your Responses" and "Discovering Your Life Themes, Patterns, and Action Steps" (not your entire prayer book). Write any insights that he or she shares with you in the space that follows on page 298. Don't forget to thank this person and to thank God for the information he reveals to you through this person. And, be patient with yourself as you digest what you have heard and move forward with what you know to be truth and God's will for your life.

# You Did It!

Congratulations! You have devoted yourself to a prayerful time of allowing God to reveal his purposes for your life. More than likely, some of the daily exercises were not easy; others may have been exhilarating. You may be filled with conflicting emotions (shock, sadness, doubt, joy, expectancy) about what you have learned and heard from God during the past sixty-plus days.

You may even need to revisit some or all of the daily questions. If so, ask God for fresh insight or for his power to guide you through your fear issues, character changes, spiritual growth spurts, a new crisis, or a unique assignment. Each time you pray about a given topic as you seek truth, you are apt to be amazed at the depth of your new understanding. Perhaps without even realizing it, you will be raising your awareness of who you were meant to be.

For today, I encourage you to move forward with what you do know—one action step after the other, until you've traveled many miles down the pathway to purpose. God will bless your obedience to his will for your life. My prayer is that you will enjoy your journey and give God all the glory for who he is, who he is helping you to become, and what he is able to accomplish through you.

# Fresh Start with Jesus

*Therefore God exalted him [Jesus] to the highest place*
*and gave him the name that is above every name,*
*that at the name of Jesus every knee should bow,*
*in heaven and on earth and under the earth,*
*and every tongue confess that Jesus Christ is Lord,*
*to the glory of God the Father.*

(Philippians 2:9-11)

Over the course of reading this book, have you agreed to let Jesus be your Savior? If you are ready to take the first step today on the pathway to purpose, here's a simple prayer you can say:

*Jesus, I believe that you died for me and that God raised you from the dead. Please forgive my sins. You are my Savior. You are my only hope. I want to follow your will for my life. I bow and confess that you, Jesus Christ, are Lord.*

If you decided just now to accept Jesus as your Savior and Lord, you are assured forever of salvation. Nothing can snatch you now from the hand of God. Please let someone know about your decision, so he or she can encourage you and thank God for his grace-filled, purposeful plan for your life.

If you decided not to say the prayer, I urge you to mark this page and to keep seeking truth with an open heart and mind. If you need help, ask a pastor or a Christian friend. Some Scripture verses that I highly recommend are these:

| | |
|---|---|
| Romans 3:23 | All have sinned. |
| Romans 6:23 | Heaven is a free gift. |
| Romans 5:8 | Jesus has already, out of love for you, paid the penalty for your sins by dying on the cross. |
| Romans 10:9–10 | If you confess that Jesus is Lord, and if you tell God that you believe he raised Jesus from the dead, you will be saved. |
| Romans 10:13 | Ask God to save you by his grace. He will! |

# ACKNOWLEDGMENTS

I am forever grateful to my son, Andy, who has been my e-commerce consultant, and who constantly asked, "How are you doing, Mom? How can I help?"

To my daughter-in-love, Julie, who is among my greatest cheerleaders, always saying, "I'm so proud of you!"

To my sweet daughter, Steph, who daily inquired, "Do you need anything from the store? Can I get you anything to eat? Can I do that for you?"

I also thank the staff administrators at Golden Gate Baptist Theological Seminary and my seminary professors who taught me to think hermeneutically.

I owe so much to the founder of LifePlanning™, Tom Paterson. Tom and Doug Slaybaugh, a pastor and friend, have both been the Holy Spirit's lifeline to my discovery of my own unique life purpose. And, I'm afraid that I can never fully express my appreciation to Catherine Dubé, who said, "Don't worry, Katie. God is never one second early or late," and to the Saddleback Church Spiritual Growth Team and staff, especially Judy Thompson, Deirdre Cantrell, Anette Rihovsky, Connie Hiss, Dawn Marriccino, Kerri Johnson, Jean Bushong, Terri Haymaker, Mary Scherff, and Pastor Lance Witt. All of them prayed for me on good days and bad.

With indebtedness, I want to thank my agent, Nancy Jernigan, whose incredible vision for the Pathway to Purpose series far surpassed my own; my editor, Cindy Hays Lambert, who is a remarkably gifted writer and tremendously insightful Christian woman. And the first-class Zondervan team, all of whom ministered to me with their kindnesses and expertise.

*The Purpose series from bestselling author Katie Brazelton*
*for women searching to find their true purpose in life*

All Purpose series books work together to enhance a woman's journey as she searches for her God-given purpose. Each book provides its own unique benefit that enriches her walk down the pathway.

*Pathway to Purpose for Women* takes the five universal purposes from *The Purpose Driven Life®* and helps women drill down to their own unique life purposes.

*Praying for Purpose for Women* is a 60-day prayer experience that can change a woman's life forever. Sixty influential Christian women share how their lives have changed.

*Conversations on Purpose for Women* is a companion book specifically designed for women who want to partner with other women to help them down the path toward purpose.

*Character Makeover* is a deeply personal 40-day journey of developing your complete character to become the best "you" God intended you to be.

| | | |
|---|---|---|
| *Pathway to Purpose for Women* | Softcover | 978-0-310-29249-4 |
| *Pathway to Purpose for Women* | Audio CD, Abridged | 978-0-310-26505-4 |
| *Pathway to Purpose for Women* | Audio Download, Abridged | 978-0-310-26857-4 |
| *Praying for Purpose for Women* | Softcover | 978-0-310-29284-5 |
| *Conversations on Purpose for Women* | Spiral | 978-0-310-25650-2 |
| *Character Makeover* | Softcover | 978-0-310-25653-3 |

Spanish products also available

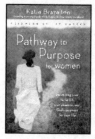
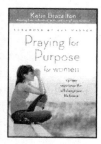

# How to Contact the Author

To learn more about **Katie Brazelton, PhD, MDiv, MA,** bestselling author, Life Coach, and founder of Life Purpose Coaching Centers International®, and her dream of opening 200 Life Purpose Coaching Centers globally...

Visit her website: www.LifePurposeCoachingCenters.com

Email her at:
WomensInfo@LifePurposeCoachingCenters.com or
MensInfo@LifePurposeCoachingCenters.com.

Write to:
Life Purpose Coaching Centers Intl
P.O. Box 80550-0550
Rancho Santa Margarita, CA 92688

Or, to invite Katie to give a life-changing keynote speech (with her special touch of humor!) to your organization, contact Ambassador Speakers Bureau in Tennessee:
(615) 370-4700
Naomi@AmbassadorSpeakers.com

\* \* \*

Katie has been a featured guest for radio and television broadcasts, such as Midday Connection and 100 Huntley Street. She has been interviewed and/or written articles for publications such as *Today's Christian Woman, Extraordinary Women,* and *Alive!* and she has been honored to speak at such venues as Focus on the Family and the American Association of Christian Counselor's (AACC) World Conference. She is an instructor on AACC's "Life Coaching DVD Series." In addition, she facilitates private, 2-day-intensive, strategic Life Purpose Plans for women leaders.

CPSIA information can be obtained at www.ICGtesting.com
Printed in the USA
LVOW07s1914140516

487836LV00021B/92/P